HOUSE...... ......No. 44.

REPORTS OF COMMISSIONERS

ON THE

HOURS OF LABOR.

Appointed under Chapter 92 of the Resolves of 1866.

BOSTON:
WRIGHT & POTTER, STATE PRINTERS,
No. 4 Spring Lane.
1867.

Commonwealth of Massachusetts.

EXECUTIVE DEPARTMENT, BOSTON,
Jan. 11, 1867.

To the House of Representatives.

I have the honor to submit, for the information of the General Court, the Reports of the Commissioners on the Hours of Labor, appointed under chapter 92 of the Resolves of 1866.

ALEX. H. BULLOCK.

Commonwealth of Massachusetts.

STATE HOUSE, BOSTON, Jan. 1, 1867.

To His Excellency Alexander H. Bullock.

The Commissioners appointed in accordance with the following Resolve of the legislature, passed May 28th, 1866,

Resolved, That a commission of three persons be appointed by the governor on or before the first day of June next, with power to send for persons and papers, to investigate the subject of the hours of labor, especially in its relation to the social, educational and sanitary condition of the industrial classes, and to the permanent prosperity of the productive interests of the State,

REPORT:

Upon entering on the duties assigned us, we referred to the report and documents of the previous Commission on the Hours of Labor, submitted to the legislature at its last session, and were happy to find that much of the labor that would otherwise have devolved upon us, had already been performed in a very satisfactory manner; and therefore confined ourselves to such additional investigations as were deemed necessary.

Circulars to the number of 450 were sent to corporations and individuals engaged in the different branches of manufacturing and mechanical industry in various parts of the Commonwealth, making the following inquiries:—

1. How many persons are employed in your works?
2. How many are females?

3. How many under the age of ten years ?
4. How many between the ages of ten and fourteen ?
5. How many *in all* under the age of eighteen years ?
6. How many children under fifteen years receive the amount of schooling required by the laws of the Commonwealth ?
7. What are the hours of labor in your establishment ?
8. How would a reduction of time to ten hours affect production ?
9. How would it operate to run your machinery with two sets of hands, eight hours each, provided sufficient laborers could be obtained ?
10. Do the social and sanitary interests of operatives, especially minors, require a reduction of the time of labor to ten hours per day ?
11. Have you tables showing the rates of wages for a series of years ? If so, for how long a period ?
12. Have wages advanced or receded within the last twenty years ?
13. Have wages advanced since 1860 ? and if so, how much ?

Another circular was sent to persons connected with, or supposed to represent, the laboring classes. To this last we shall have occasion to refer at the close of this Report.

The answers returned to the questions, what number of persons are employed, and how many are females ? we have found sufficiently explicit; but to our inquiries how many are under the age of ten years and between ten and fourteen years ? the answers have been very imperfect and unsatisfactory. From the nature of the case, we must suppose this unavoidable. Employers have no means of determining the question of age, and often have no motive to do so ; and parents are frequently interested in representing their children to be older than they really are, in order to secure employment for them, and obtain a higher rate of wages. For these reasons little reliance can be placed upon the returns made in regard to persons employed under fourteen years of age, and from our own personal observation we are well persuaded that the number of such is far greater than would be indicated in any statistics now obtainable. We know that there is a general, but, we are happy to say, not universal, disregard of that part of the Act of 1866, chapter 273, section 1, which says, " no child under ten years of age shall be employed in any manufacturing establishment within this Commonwealth." We believe that thousands of these victims of cupidity and avarice are so employed at this moment, and their condition deserves the attention of the executive and legislative departments of the government.

If we are asked, how it happens that this positive enactment is disregarded, we reply, that when we have asked the superintendent of the mill, for example, why he employed such children, his ready answer would be, " I do not employ such ; they are employed by the overseers of the rooms." The second section of the law to which we have referred says, " The *owner*, *agent* or *superintendent* of any manufacturing establishment who knowingly employs a child in violation of the preceding section shall forfeit a sum not exceeding fifty dollars for each offence."

Now as the overseer of a room, and many other subordinates in factories, who contract with and employ those under their direction, are not in express terms either *owner*, *agent or superintendent*, it is deemed a safe evasion of the law in question, as there is no one to whom it attaches. To make the law effective, it is only needful that it be so amended as to read, " the owner, agent or superintendent of any manufacturing establishment who allows a child to be employed in violation of the preceding section shall forfeit a sum not exceeding fifty dollars for each offence ; " to which we think the clause should be added, *one-half of which shall go to the complainant*. This is desirable to secure a prosecution, as such a proceeding always involves a responsibility few are willing to assume without consideration.

But the Commissioners are entirely satisfied as to the result of their own observation and inquiries, that no laws or regulations, however wise and humane, will afford protection to the laboring classes, unless they have an *official friend*, to whom they can appeal with confidence, and whose sole duty is to see that their rights are respected, and the laws made in their behalf executed. And this officer must be entirely independent of popular suffrage. He must receive his appointment from the executive, and be responsible to him for his conduct. And hence we earnestly recommend that it be made the duty of the governor to appoint such an officer. And to avoid the multiplication of different departments of service, it seems to us that if the governor were authorized to assign one of the State constabulary as SPECIAL INSPECTOR OF LABOR, whose duty should be to see to the execution of all laws made in its behalf, and report his doings to the executive annually or oftener as deemed most expedient, the object would be attained in a cheap yet effective manner; and if the law should further authorize such inspector to call on the State constabulary for any additional assistance he might need, the great object would be secured with but little difficulty.

We do not presume, however, to go into details in regard to the law, or the execution of it, but the fact that such an inspector of labor has become a great and pressing necessity, we wish to urge most strongly upon the attention of the government.

MINORS.

To our fifth inquiry, "How many in all under eighteen years of age?" we have received sufficiently definite replies. In a large part of our heavier mechanic establishments, but few if any minors are employed, but in our woollen and cotton mills they are found in large numbers. In twenty-five of the most considerable of these, we obtain the following result:—

Whole number of hands, ... 25,842
Under 18 years of age, ... 4,985

Nearly one-fifth, or 19.29 per cent. It is our opinion, however, that the proportion is considerably greater than these figures indicate. In many, and indeed in most cases, the returns must be mere estimates on the part of those who made them, from the want of any accurate knowledge of the actual age of their employees, and for the reasons before given, many would be reported as over eighteen who were actually under that age. We should think it probable that the true proportion was not less than 25 per cent.

But taking even the lowest rate per cent., we perceive what an immense number of minors must be employed in the aggregate, in the numerous industrial establishments of the Commonwealth, and that their interests may well demand the attention of the government.

To the sixth question, in regard to the schooling of children, answers were generally returned, and we shall have occasion to refer to them, when called to speak upon the interests of education.

Hours of Labor.

Answers to the seventh inquiry were received from seventy-four establishments, which give the following as the hours of labor:—

5 worked 10¾ hours.
63 "   11 hours.
4 "   12 hours.
12 "   irregular hours, 8 to 15.

From this it will be seen that eleven hours is the rule, and any shorter or longer time the exception in the factories of the Commonwealth.

This fact brings before us one of the most important considerations connected with the industrial interests of the State.

Our cotton and woollen mills, employing a large proportion of women and children, are run for eleven hours each day, while our mechanic shops in general, in which no females, and but few children are employed, are kept in operation but ten hours.

While we are happy to bear our testimony to the excellent character of most of the cotton and woollen mills we have visited, while the larger ones especially are well built, well ventilated and cleanly kept, we have been satisfied from our personal observation, as well as the testimony of those best qualified to judge, that eleven hours' toil each day for six days in each week, is more than women and children ought to be required to perform. We are certain that they cannot do this without imparing, sooner or later, their vital powers, and shortening the duration of life. We are confident that it is a most uneconomical waste of life, which it is the interest of the State to prevent.

How great that interest is, may be seen from the limited statistics we now present:—

In sixty-five concerns there were employed in all, 33,000 hands.

Of these, there were females, ... 19,746
or 60 per cent.

In twelve of the largest cotton mills we found,—

Number of hands, ... 19,979
of females, ... 12,977
About 65 per cent.

As some of these mills had print-works, and employed a large number of males, we are of the opinion, that in the strictly cotton manufacturing business there must be at least two-thirds, or say 67 per cent. If to these we should add the male children under eighteen years of age, the number of which we have no means of determining, we should probably find the number of women and children equal to seventy-five per cent. of the whole number of persons employed. In our earliest examinations in relation to the hours of labor we were painfully impressed with the feeling that this large class of persons ought to be relieved, if possible, from the hardships of a condition which compels them to work sixty-six hours per week. We were soon led to conclude that unless there existed the most imperative necessity for such extended hours of service, all under eighteen years of age ought to be restricted to ten hours per day.

One of the first considerations presented was that the hours of labor in this country must conform, in a good degree, to the hours of labor in that country from which we find our greatest rivalry as a manufacturing people ; and accordingly, soon after our Commission was formed, one of our number wrote for information in regard to the hours of labor in Great Britain, to Elihu Burritt, Esq., the American Consular Agent at Birmingham. To the inquiries proposed, a prompt answer was returned, from which we give the following extracts :—

"It may be fairly assumed that the ten-hour system is established in England universally amongst all trades and occupations, and that every one is paid for all work over that time. In the great Labor Congress at Geneva, composed of representatives from nearly all countries, the English delegates advocated nine hours, as a standard day's work, but they did not carry it. The system in Birmingham is very generous and accommodating to the workmen. They go into the factory, or shop, at eight, and work till one, which makes five hours; they then go to dinner and resume work at two, and labor until seven; a half hour being allowed them at five o'clock for TEA, which is made in the factory. There is generally a boiler provided by the proprietors, and their porter boils the water for the men and women, who make their tea in their own dinner mugs, and pour it into their tea-cups, which they furnish themselves. You will notice that the half hour at tea is taken from the ten, so that the laborers work only nine and a half hours a day. In summer however, they work from two till six-thirty, without stopping for tea, that they may add the half hour allowed them for it, to the long evening of leisure.

"You will see how much more lenient and generous this system is, than the one adopted in New England, where men, women, and children, are *belled* up from their beds in the winter while it is yet dark, to eat their breakfast by candle-light, and work by candle-light at both ends of the day. * * There is a great deal to be learned in England by our manufacturers in regard to the rights of labor. One thing I would urge upon you —to keep a sharp look-out for *factory children.* You know that the English government has factory inspectors, who travel about and keep a sharp watch on the manufacturers, and see that the humane laws are carried out, which prevent children from being dragged into the factories under a certain age, and without schooling. It will require the keenest vigilance in New England to prevent this tendency to create an ignorant, spiritless and helpless factory population.

"For the credit of Massachusetts, of which we are all so proud, I hope you will look closely into these matters; lest while our people are bragging of their freedom and enlightenment, a great and constantly increasing class among us will sink lower and lower in the scale of mental, moral and physical well-being. * * The hungry avidity for large dividends, the concentration of capital, and the intangibility and invisibility of stockholders, all operate in one direction, both in sentiment and policy, and you must lift up a standard against it. * * Could not the Massachusetts legislature be induced to appoint an inspector of factories, such as we have here?"

In addition to the facts and opinions derived from the returns, we have visited a large number of industrial establishments, factories and workshops in different parts of the Commonwealth, and from conversations with those who had the charge of them, we are satisfied that they would readily acquiesce in the proposed reduction.

A Law for the Protection of Minors.

While we do not recommend to your Excellency that any law be passed interfering with the hours of adult laborers, who can choose their own employments, we earnestly recommend that a law be enacted similar to that of Great Britain, that no person under eighteen years of age shall be employed more than ten hours each day, or sixty hours per week. That such a law, the rightfulness of which we think no one can well dispute, would cause a general reduction in the hours of labor for *all* employed in factories, as well as minors, we have no doubt. Such was the effect in England, very fortunately, and such would unquestionably be the result here.

A very great amelioration of the condition of the British laborer has taken place within the last twenty years, but it required the efforts of the humane and philanthropic for the previous thirty years to accomplish it. The history of the great struggle,* published in two volumes, now in our State library, is one of intense interest, and well deserves the careful study of those who would know the terrible thraldom from which the operatives of Great Britain have been emancipated. The condition of the laboring classes was shocking almost beyond belief; but the amount of suffering, the destruction of human life, and the moral and mental degradation it entailed upon the masses, were disregarded until the friends of humanity interfered; and then it required a tedious contest for one whole generation to induce the government to interfere in the laborer's behalf; but when it did so it was with effect. This is characteristic of the British government, which, proverbially slow to enact any law making essential changes in the social or political condition of the country, is quite sure to execute any law which it places upon the statute book.

* Alfred's History of the Factory Movement.

The testimony which Mr. Burritt has given us in regard to the greatly improved condition of British operatives, is highly encouraging and satisfactory, since it comes from one who has spent a great part of the last twenty years in England, and travelled more extensively, and become more intimately acquainted with the people of that country, than perhaps any other American.

But we are not restricted to the testimony of this gentleman, however full or satisfactory it may be. A large number of documents appertaining to the subject have been kindly forwarded to us from England, all confirming his statements, and showing how highly satisfactory the changes which have been made are, both to the workmen and their employers. We could make extracts from these publications that would fill a volume, all of which would go to prove that the new policy adopted in England is not only highly beneficial to the industrial prosperity of the country, but to its social and moral interests.

In reply to our eighth inquiry, "How would a reduction of time to ten hours affect production?" we have generally received the answer, "*In the same ratio*," or "one-eleventh."

That the adoption of ten instead of eleven hours would reduce the immediate production of goods we readily grant; not indeed to the precise extent of one-eleventh, as some manufacturers have assumed, but doubtless nearly to that extent. This at the present time would be an advantage rather than otherwise; but we do not admit that in the long run anything would be lost to production, for several decided benefits would be derived from this course.

1. The operatives would be more able to perform ten than eleven hours' labor, and would work more profitably to their employers.

2. There would be a great deal less of lost time. As it now is, these minors often get jaded out by their long hours of labor, and are compelled of necessity to lay by for a few days, and after awhile to leave the business for months or years to recruit. This fact is well known to manufacturers.

3. By reducing the hours, employers are certain to get a higher grade of laborers, more able and intelligent hands.

As *some* mills now are, there is an evident deterioration in the character of those employed. None can be had to work in them, except the most dependent families. If the time was reduced as proposed, it would operate as a powerful inducement for many of a better class to work in the mill who now refuse to do so. The last hour of the eleven implies more hardship than two hours in the previous ten would do.

That all the best interests of operatives would be promoted by such a reduction, is acknowledged by many of the largest and best manufacturers in the country.

In reply to question No. 10, " Do the social and sanitary interests of operatives, especially minors, require a reduction of the time of labor to ten hours per day ? " Hon. Amos A. Lawrence gives the following answer : " Yes. The physical, intellectual, moral and religious interests of our people require a reduction. The present system of labor is debasing the native New England stock, and forcing them to emigrate to the West, South, and foreign countries. The population which displaces ours is inferior in every respect."

In a note accompanying the return, Mr. Lawrence adds : " On the main question of work within doors, and especially the employment of children, I have believed for thirty years that our practice was bad." From the agent of the Pacific Mills (employing 3,800 hands,) to whom we are indebted for very full and satisfactory replies, and who has given his views at length on both sides of the question, showing the objections to and the arguments for such a reduction, we have the following conclusion : " On the whole, I should be very willing to have the experiment tried, and should use my influence to give it, as far as I might be concerned, a fair trial. This being had, I would gladly abide by its obvious results."

From the Hamilton Company, at Lowell, we have the following : " In my judgment, the social and sanitary interests of all would be materially advanced by such a reduction."

Others, again, reply that the reduction would be desirable, provided the system were extended throughout New England.

In answer to this it may be said, that if Massachusetts adopted the ten-hour rule, other States would doubtless feel compelled to follow. Such has been the case hitherto. Once the factories of Massachusetts ran for twelve or thirteen hours daily. As they have been gradually reduced to eleven, other communities have fallen into the same limit; and now when it is proposed to establish ten hours, there seems to be the best of reasons for believing that such would become the general rule throughout the country.

It is very gratifying to be able to state at this point, that several of the largest mills in some of our most important manufacturing cities have, since the organization of this Commission, voluntarily reduced their hours of labor to ten each day, or sixty hours per week.

In reply to our ninth question, "How would it operate to run your machinery with two sets of hands, eight hours each, provided sufficient laborers could be obtained?" we have received generally the answer we expected; viz., that it would be, in most cases, impracticable. Many kinds of manufactures are of such a character that the change could not be made, though in others there would be little difficulty. That a great object would be attained if capital or investments could be made to work sixteen hours, while human beings were obliged to labor but eight, will be admitted by all; and that such a consummation will be ultimately reached, seems very possible, but at present the experiment is rather a matter of anticipation than anything to be practically attempted.

The subject of our tenth inquiry, whether the social and sanitary condition of operatives, especially minors, requires a reduction of the time of labor to ten hours each day, has been anticipated to some extent in our consideration of the seventh question.

The answers given have varied greatly. Many are directly and positively in the negative; others as directly in the affirmative; others, still, are conditional, that is, "provided the operatives would make a good use of their additional leisure," of which many express a strong doubt. In regard to this last point, we suppose that the answers given have been influenced by the social condition of the general population in which the establishment is situated. In those well-ordered communities, where no places of demoralization are permitted, the reply would naturally be, that the additional leisure hour would be an advantage, because it would be well spent; while in those

1867.] HOUSE—No. 44. 15

of an opposite character, the reply would come very emphatically in the negative.

That the *sanitary condition* of factory operatives would be greatly improved by a reduction of one hour each day, we think no reasonable man can deny; but this point has been so fully and ably discussed in the report of the previous Commission on the Hours of Labor, and in various documents before the public, that we deem it quite unnecessary to dwell upon it.

WAGES.

In connection with the hours of labor, we extended our inquiries (as they could be made without appreciable labor or expense,) to the cognate question of WAGES, which it is well known have changed greatly within the last five years. All classes are so much interested in this matter that we deemed it not inappropriate to submit the question, *how much have wages advanced since* 1860? Answers to this inquiry have been returned from 102 establishments, including in their employ 39,216 persons, from which it appears that the average rate in all these is 63.2 per cent. advance since 1860. But there is much reason to believe that this average is rather above the actual advance. First, because the statements and general conclusions arrived at have been in many cases estimates, though based on actual figures to a great extent. Secondly, because the natural bias of the employer who makes the returns, would be likely to influence him to overstate rather than understate the wages of those in his employ, since the higher the rate of wages the greater his own generosity.

As a proof in point, it may be stated, that one manufacturing firm returned the advance in wages since 1860, at "75 to 200 per cent." Thinking this an extravagant and very indefinite statement, we wrote for an explanation, and desired that the *average rate* for all the workmen should be carefully ascertained. We received in reply that, "*the average advance as taken from our pay-rolls, is* 52 *per cent.*" The average by the first statement was 137½. We are fully of the opinion that many of the replies made to this inquiry were equally conjectural, though not so extravagant.

Thirdly, because the quality or value of labor is constantly improving. For example, (as we found on inquiry,) a hand whose wages were $1.50 in 1860, now receives $3.25 per day, yet had this same person been as good a workman in 1860 as he is in 1866, his work then would have been worth $2.25 ; so that his actual wages, instead of having advanced something more than 130 per cent., have advanced, taking the actual quality of his labor into account, but about 45 per cent., the balance being attributable to the improved quality of his work. The principle involved in this case applies to a large part of all the skilled labor of the Commonwealth, and must raise considerably the average rate of the whole. None of the considerations enumerated should be disregarded in determining the question how much wages have advanced since 1860.

Although no official investigation has been made by us in regard to the wages of labor in other departments of industry, yet, from somewhat extended inquiries made by one of our number, it is believed that the advance in farm labor has been about the same as that of factory laborers. In regard to the labor of females as domestics in families, it is believed to have generally advanced since 1860 but about one-third, though in the large towns and cities the advance may have been as high as fifty per cent. Probably forty per cent. would be the highest average advance that could be stated for female labor in household employments.

From these premises, we conclude that the average advance in wages of all kinds of labor throughout the State is about 50 per cent. In the meantime, as it is well known that commodities have, for three years past, been raised in price 100 per cent. or more,* it will be seen that the laboring

---

* These estimates of the rise of wages and commodities we find to accord very well with the Report of the Special Commissioner of the Revenue, Hon. D. A. Wells, December, 1866. He says :—

"In Massachusetts the increase of mechanics' wages is 60 per cent., while that of all the employees of the State, male and female, and including farm laborers, is 50 per cent."

Mr. Wells' estimate of the rise in *prices* is 85 per cent. But we must notice that these are "wholesale prices," not the prices at which the laborer had to purchase his commodities. Of course the latter had to pay the additional profits of the jobber and retailer upon the 85 per cent. extra price, so that the cost to him must have been, as we have just stated, "100 per cent. or more!" On page 62 of Mr. Wells' Report, an instance is given where an actual investigation was made, and it was found that, while wages had advanced 55 to 60 per cent., commodities had advanced about 130 per cent.

classes must have suffered greatly from this difference between the rise of their wages and the rise of prices. That they have been compelled to deprive themselves of many of their accustomed enjoyments, is certain. They have less to expend for food and clothing, for amusement and culture. They have been amongst the greatest sufferers from a redundant and, consequently, depreciated currency. But this is a misfortune from which it is not possible for the legislature of Massachusetts to relieve them, except by its influence upon the National Government, in favor of a return to a sound standard of value.

Rate of Wages for a Series of Years.

It will be observed by your Excellency that, in the eleventh of our inquiries, we have asked the question, " Have you tables showing the rate of wages *for a series of years*, — if so, for how long a period ?" To this, we have received replies to the effect, in some cases, that such tables or pay-rolls are in existence as would make it quite practicable to obtain the rate of wages, in many cases, for twenty years. There is no doubt in our minds, that statistics for the last fifty years might be obtained without difficulty, showing what the wages of labor have been in every department of industry, — agricultural, mechanical and manufacturing; and what the variations in those wages have been during that time ; what has been the cause of such variations, and whether the prices of commodities have corresponded with the fluctuations in the rate of wages. A table showing the prices of a large number of staple articles from the year 1825 to 1863, has been carefully prepared and published by the Treasury Department at Washington (see Financial Report, 1863,) so that by ascertaining, as we can easily do, the rate of wages for a corresponding period, we may determine with great accuracy in how far the laboring classes have been affected by the fluctuations in prices; and, what is equally important, we may discover the causes of such fluctuations.

We are strongly impressed with the conviction that a bureau ought to be established in this Commonwealth, to collect statistics of every kind in relation to the industry and social condition of the people. At present we have but few statistics relating to the affairs of the State, and these few are exceedingly imperfect and unreliable. Our decennial statistics of industry are very far from affording that accurate information which is needed to secure useful results; and but few of the actual teachings, which such statistics should afford for practical use, are brought out and made apparent.

We need the undivided attention and efforts of at least one competent person to carry out this important measure.

Time allowed for Dinner.

There is another subject in this connection, to which we beg leave to call the attention of your Excellency, which, however trivial it may seem to those who have never had occasion to reflect upon it, is one of sufficient importance in the eyes of the Commissioners, and in the hearts of thousands of operatives in Massachusetts, to deserve the attention of the government. We allude to the amount of time allowed for dinner. In no small share of the mills, this time is restricted to forty-five minutes. In that short period the operatives must leave the mills, make their way to their homes or boarding-houses, prepare themselves for their meal, eat it, and get back to their places in the factory. In many cases they must go a distance of half to three-quarters of a mile each way. And three-fourths of those who thus struggle for their dinner are *women* and *children*, many of the latter under ten or twelve years of age!

Now, what they ask, what humanity demands, is that the law shall say that one hour at least shall in all cases be allowed for dinner. It can be seen at once that nobody will be made poorer by this arrangement, that the production of the mills will not be reduced by a farthing, that no one will be injured or incommoded. Fifteen minutes thus gained will nearly double the actual time the operatives now have in which to take their meals; for a great part of all the time at present allowed them, is spent in going to and returning from their places of labor.

Education.

The State very properly assumes the right to provide that all its children shall be furnished with the means of education; and for years has required that chidren of tender age, shall not be employed in factories, unless they have attended school a certain number of months in each year. The law enacted last year increased the number of months to six, which in some towns covers all the time in which schools are maintained. We have no means of knowing how well the law is enforced. We have reason to suppose in some cases, when children are out of the factories for the purpose, they do not attend school.

The graduated tables of the board of education for 1865, show that 162 towns and cities, giving an average attendance of from $75\frac{98}{100}$ to 100, are mostly small farming towns, only twelve having over one thousand children each; but of these, three, Lowell, Waltham and Fitchburg are manufacturing towns, where a good degree of care for educating their children is manifest. These 162 towns and cities have but 80,488 of the 247,217, the whole number returned in the State between five and fifteen, and have a mean average attendance of 65,965. The last two pages of the table show that the average attendance is not so large in the larger towns and cities; the rate being from $43\frac{81}{100}$ to $75\frac{95}{100}$. In thirteen manufacturing towns, 28,880 children have a mean average attendance of 16,166. In twenty-four farming towns, 6,709 children show an attendance of 4,438. This may be explained in part from the fact that more private schools exist in the larger towns, and that in the manufacturing towns a portion of the children are released from labor to attend school one season of the year, and another part at a different season.

There seems now to be no adequate mode of ascertaining how well the law requiring children to attend school so many months in the year is observed. In some towns no persons will take the position of truant officer, and when the duty is imposed upon the school committee or other officer, it is imperfectly performed, or neglected altogether.

The law of the last session authorized the governor to appoint, by the advice of the council, a State constable who should see to the enforcement of the laws with regard to the ages of children employed in factories and their attendance upon school.

The relation of the hours of labor to the moral, the sanitary, the intellectual as well as the productive interests of the State, is intimately connected with the education of the children of the State. One officer cannot do the whole work; but with the co-operation of the local State constables and the school committees, one perfectly qualified officer to see that the work is done, is what is needed and should be positively required.

When the school committee of one of our wealthiest towns, making the largest appropriations for its schools by the scholar, report that " truant officers were chosen at the annual meeting of the town, but they declined to serve ; at the adjourned meeting others were chosen, but with no better success ; the result has been, we have been without a truant officer and truants have governed themselves accordingly ;"—the necessity for a State officer becomes apparent. Local authorities cannot be relied upon at all times to enforce wholesome regulations.

The reduction of the hours of labor cannot prove a benefit without it is accompanied by increased intelligence and skill. We must educate our children to fit them for something more than the drudgery of labor. With the increased skill and intelligence of the laborer, the improvements of machinery and the increase of wealth, the desire and the capacity to enjoy leisure will surely come, and the desire will be gratified.

Thus far we are happy to state to your Excellency, that all our conclusions have been entirely harmonious, and we are equally earnest in the recommendations made ; but on the remaining point to be considered, viz. : whether the legislature should be invoked to enact a law fixing the hours of labor for mechanics at eight hours, instead of ten, as now in general practice, the undersigned feel compelled to differ so widely from their colleague, as to make it expedient that each party should present a separate report. But in parting with him at this point, the undersigned beg leave to bear their cordial testimony to the zeal and fidelity with which he has discharged the duties assigned him, and to his earnest devotion to the welfare of his fellow workingmen.

For convenience we give the following recapitulation of the different recommendations mentioned in the foregoing pages of this Report.

1. That the Act of the last session, chapter 273, be so amended as to insure the execution of those provisions which forbid the employment of children between the ages of ten and fourteen, and provides for their attendance at school.

2. That the employment of all persons under the age of eighteen years in factories, for more than ten hours each day, or sixty hours per week, be prohibited, and that one hour each day shall be allowed for dinner.

3. That a special INSPECTOR OF LABOR be appointed, to see that all laws relating to the interests of the laboring classes are faithfully executed.

4. That a Bureau of Statistics be established for the purpose of collecting and making available all facts relating to the industrial and social interests of the Commonwealth.

THE EIGHT-HOUR MOVEMENT.

A very extended movement amongst the leading workingmen of this country and Europe is now being made in favor of a reduction of the hours of labor from ten to eight each day. The government of this Commonwealth is called upon to aid in this reduction, by the enactment of a law restricting the hours of labor.

That the movement is one of vast importance if successful, there can be no doubt. It will relieve the laboring class of one-fifth part of their present toil, and, of consequence, greatly affect the production of wealth; since it will not, it is presumed, be seriously contended, that as much wealth can be created in eight hours as in ten; especially when, as is generally the case at the present day, labor is connected with machinery which moves at a certain speed, irrespective of the hours in which it is operated. The subject is one of such magnitude that it seems desirable to present the following

GENERAL CONSIDERATIONS.

The most industrious races of men are the most intelligent and powerful, the most elevated, mentally and morally. Those countries where severe and continuous labor is required for the support of life, are the most prosperous and progressive, and exert the widest influence. On the other hand, where there is the least demand for human effort to sustain existence, as in tropical countries, where leisure rather than labor is the rule of life, we find the greatest demoralization, and the lowest standard of civilization.

Man rises in proportion as his necessities are great, as his labor is constant; he sinks when his absolute wants can be met with little exertion. All this is too patent in the history of the world, and the common observation of all men, to need proof.

Work, then, is a blessing; idleness, or exemption from labor, a curse. Man was made for work,—his happiness, his intellectual growth and physical development depend upon it.

Another fact presents itself. Those who are compelled to labor hard for the common necessaries of life, are the most certain to be constantly increasing in their desires. When one gratification is secured, another still is wanted, and men are found ever ready to make additional efforts to secure additional gratifications. There seems to be no limit to the desires of such persons for the objects that industry alone can create. Quite otherwise is it with those whose necessities are met with but little labor. Their desires are stationary, and they make little progress.

These are suggestive facts, and have much to do with the question of the hours of labor. They show that exemption from toil is not for the welfare of mankind, but they do not prove that men may not be compelled by their desires to work too hard, and for a greater length of time than their best interests may require.

Again, all wealth, being created by labor acting in conjunction with capital, (which is but accumulated labor employed in reproduction,) the greater, other things equal, the amount of labor, the greater will be the sum of enjoyments which may be possessed by man. But while this is true, it is certain that men may labor so severely and incessantly, as in the long run to impair the vital energies, and thus reduce the powers of production; and it may be further true, that too great an amount of toil may not only injure the physical powers, but depress or impair the mental faculties, so that in this way the productive capacity of a people may be greatly lessened. And still further, not only the physical and mental, but the moral nature of man may be imbruted by severe and unreasonably protracted toil. All this being apparent, the question of the hours that should constitute a day's labor, is one deserving of a careful and candid examination. The great point to be aimed at in the culture of a people, is to secure the highest production of wealth, consistent with preserving intact all the natural powers of the laborer, and advancing his best and highest interests, his full and complete manhood.

We have said that idleness was a curse ; but leisure, a relief from toil, is not uncommonly even more so. Whether it is so or not, depends entirely upon the use that is made of it. If the laborer, after he has performed a given amount of effort, spends the rest of his time in healthy recreation, in acquiring useful knowledge, in moral and intellectual culture ; or if he has a family, in the education and training of his children, his leisure will be a blessing to himself and to others If on the other hand, the hours of exemption from toil are wasted in idle and vicious amusements, the less leisure he has the better.

The desirableness and even the necessity for leisure, however, increases with the increase of the responsibilities of the citizen. A laborer in the United States needs more leisure, or relief from toil, than one in the same position in Europe, because he has the elective franchise, and is a part of the government. If he is deficient in intellectual training and moral culture, the State will suffer. The American laborer must not only take care of himself, but discharge his civil duties and fulfil his obligations to the interests of religion and morality. This responsibility involves the necessity of intelligence and culture, and these require leisure and opportunity. It is not enough that the laborer have education in childhood ; he must have the means of constant improvement and progress in manhood. He must not only know something of the past, but be familiar with the events of the present. New ideas, new discoveries, new issues are made from day to day, and the laborer must have the means of knowing what these are. All this requires time, and not only time, but rest from toil in such a condition that the mind can engage with its full strength in intellectual pursuits. Hence it follows that the hours devoted to labor should not be so extended as not to leave sufficient time and strength to engage in those pursuits which will qualify the laborer for the discharge of his duties to himself, his family, and his government. Great social movements are in continual progress—these, the American laborer ought not only to be cognizant of, but take a part in ; yet whether he shall do so efficiently and intelligently or not, must clearly depend upon two conditions: first, that he has the necessary leisure; and secondly, that he improves that leisure for the desired purpose. The mechanics of Massachusetts, as an almost universal fact, work ten hours per day. If we allow two hours for the three meals of the day, and eight hours for sleep, we have still four hours left. Are these sufficient? and if so, is the laborer after ten hours of continuous toil, in a condition of mind and body adapted to the profitable improvement of these hours? The necessary cares of a family, if he has one, must demand a part of his leisure moments; how much, depends upon many circumstances, as how far he is from his place of labor, and from other places which he must of necessity visit.

It will be seen, then, taking into view all these considerations, that the time left to the laborer for leisure to be devoted to personal improvement and the discharge of social and public duties, must be very limited. We should look at these facts in all their significance, and if there be anything that legislation can do to ameliorate the condition of the laborer, it certainly should be done.

Laboring men, as all have seen, ask that their hours of toil may be reduced from ten, the present limit, to eight hours per day. That they should desire such a reduction is not surprising; but the question which arises of most importance to them is, whether such a change, if practicable, would be for their best good? And another question would arise, viz., whether the change would be for the best interests of all concerned, the employer as well as the employed, the consumer as well as the producer? If these questions can be answered in the affirmative, there should be no delay in carrying out the proposed reform; for, other things equal, it is undoubtedly desirable that the hours of labor should be reduced.

The primary inquiry would seem to be, whether the laborer can get as large wages, that is, as many commodities, for the shorter as for the longer period?

To this we must answer: certainly, he will get as much wages, if he can produce as much value in eight hours as in ten, but not otherwise. The reward of the laborer, though usually paid in money (or that which by courtesy is called money,) is in fact a certain share of the commodities which he produces. The more, therefore, he can produce, the larger will be the amount of wages, since the latter must always bear a certain proportion to the former. The question therefore is, can as much be produced in eight as in ten hours? The difference between ten and eight hours is equal to a discount of one-fifth, or twenty per cent. But, as in the case of the proposed reduction of factory labor from eleven to ten hours, we do not conclude that the actual reduction in the amount produced would be in exact proportion. The last two hours would not be quite as productive as the previous eight; and we may safely answer that, instead of a loss to production of 20 per cent., the difference would be but one-sixth, or $16\tfrac{2}{3}$ per cent. This, although it is of course but an estimate, must, we feel assured, be near the truth. If so, then the loss would be just the same as working five days out of six under the ten-hour system. There would be less production of all commodities by one-sixth. Capital in all its forms must stand still to the same extent as the workman, since one cannot go on without the other. That the production of all commodities will be reduced one-sixth, when the effective hours of labor are reduced to that extent, we take it no one will dispute. If so, the laborer will have one-sixth less, and the capitalist, or he who carries on business, will, under such a reduction of time, have one-sixth less.

The question, then, of the reducing the hours of labor has two sides. The laborer is as much interested in production as the capitalist, for he is a consumer as well as producer, and, as such, is concerned in having the largest production of wealth, and in having the commodities he requires at the lowest price at which they can be afforded,—since the lower the price the greater the sum of his enjoyments. The capitalist will not encounter all the loss which a reduction of the hours of labor may cause. He furnishes capital for as many hours as the laborer does his services; why then should he suffer more than his share of the loss? There is no good reason why he should do so, and it is certain he will not.

If the laborer were to receive as much for eight as for ten hours, while he would produce but five-sixths as much, the commodities he created would of necessity be enhanced correspondingly in price. Then, if laborers form the most numerous class of society, and consume the greater part of all common products, would they not lose in additional price what they had gained by the shortening of the hours of labor? Would not the final result be that they would work less, and have less? If the laborer could get as much for eight hours as for ten, why not do better, and demand as much for *six as for eight?* or, better still, demand as much for *four as for six?* for TWO AS FOR FOUR? If the *principle* was a sound one, it would hold throughout. But we see it will not hold, because it becomes absurd, and we perceive that the attempt to make eight hours equal to ten is impracticable. This much-indulged fallacy arises in a great degree from the fact that the laborer supposes he is working for money wages, when in reality he is only working for the commodities that money will purchase. If, therefore, he raises the cost of commodities, he injures himself more than the capitalist, since all the laborer's wages, or nearly so, are generally expended for articles which he must consume in order to live. This is a consideration certainly worthy the attention of the laborer.

Again, it is further to be inquired in this connection, whether the laborer would not sacrifice that for which he would willingly work more than eight hours per day? whether he would get as many of the necessaries and luxuries of life by eight hours' labor as by ten? whether he could well afford to relinquish any considerable part of what he now enjoys, or would not rather prefer to encounter present hardships than suffer additional privations?

But still another question arises? Would the workingman spend his additional leisure in a wise and useful manner, so that it would really contribute to his elevation and improvement, or in such a way as to injure himself and family? That is a grave and pertinent inquiry. That some men would use their additional leisure, as they now use the little leisure they get, in a judicious manner, so as to make it a means of intellectual and moral elevation, there can be no doubt. There is always a certain proportion of sensible, ambitious men who are bound to succeed, and they accomplish their object by untiring assiduity and industry,—but how would it be with the majority? In answering this last inquiry, we must remember that the State makes no provision for the improvement of its people after they pass out of the public schools. They are thrown upon their own resources; neither libraries, reading rooms, or places of social resort are provided by the State, or by the church, or by society, *as a general fact;* and therefore operatives, unless they have homes of their own, are literally turned into the street, to find a place of resort and social enjoyment wherever they can; and, as there is but one place where they are always welcome, and that is the lager beer saloon or some similar beneficent institution (?), they are of necessity compelled to shut themselves up in their lodging rooms, or resort to these places of refuge.

Such being the unquestionable condition of things, it is not to be wondered that many are led to the belief, that the less leisure the working people, especially the younger part of them, have, the better. This is doubtless one of the most weighty considerations in regard to the effect of a reduction in the hours of labor, and one that we think should arrest the attention of the people of the Commonwealth. Our social condition has almost totally changed. From an agricultural and rural population in 1820, we have become a great manufacturing community, with numerous large towns and cities; and yet, in many respects, our institutions, social and religious, have remained almost unchanged. As a people we have not awakened to the exigencies of our new condition; and our means of social and intellectual improvement and culture are in no adequate proportion to the density and urban character of our population. Especially are we destitute of places of amusement of a *rational and elevating character.* We have absolutely none for the masses of the people. We seem to have no faith in any places of resort for public entertainment, except those provided by the church on the one hand, and the theatre on the other. However painful this statement of the case may be, is it not indisputably true? And if so, does it not form one of the social problems which we are called upon to solve? Yet it certainly is not a valid reason why we should keep our laboring classes shut up in shops and factories for unreasonable hours, because we have provided nothing for their improvement and entertainment when they are let out.

Society then, we perceive, has not only a direct and positive interest in the hours and condition of labor, but in the hours and conditions of leisure; and though it may not interfere with the personal liberty of these who are of an adult age, it may and ought to protect those classes who cannot determine for themselves under what circumstances, or to what extent they shall labor or recreate.

But we pass to the consideration of another question connected with the proposed change.

It has been strongly insisted that the loss arising from shortening the hours of labor, if indeed there be a loss, will fall wholly on the employer of labor.

But if we regard the point as settled, and there would seem to be no reasonable doubt in regard to it, that the laborer cannot produce as much in ten hours as in eight, then the manufacturer, for example, who could produce 60,000 yards of cassimere per annum under the ten-hour system, would, on the supposition we have made of one-sixth deficiency, now produce but 50,000, yet this quantity would cost him the same for labor as the 60,000 yards did before the change. Therefore he must raise the rate of profit upon his goods to get an equal aggregate amount.

But it may be erroneously, yet sincerely urged, that instead of this the manufacturer must take the loss, and be content with less profit. This will certainly not be the case if he can use his capital to better advantage, at home or abroad, than to continue his manufacture at the loss of a considerable part of his profits. If, from necessity, he is compelled to do this, his accumulation of capital will be reduced in proportion to the falling off of his profits. It may be thought, however, that this does not concern the *laborer*, yet it certainly does, for as the number of laborers is continually increasing by the natural increase of population, and by immigration, *capital must increase in an equal ratio*, or labor cannot find full employment, and the competition will be so great as to reduce wages. Such a result is beyond a question. The laborer in the end would be the greatest sufferer. Here we find a confirmation of the principle, that the interests of the employer and the employed are inseparably united; that one cannot be injured and the other not suffer; that both have a common interest in the profitableness of all kinds of business. They are copartners, not antagonists.

But it has been argued " that the reduction of hours which has already taken place, was not attended with a reduction of wages. The labor of mechanics in general, up to about 1840, was nominally eleven to twelve hours. The time has been reduced to ten, and wages, instead of being lower, have been raised." In reply to this we may remark that the change of hours has been gradually accomplished, occupying a quarter of a century; and during that period there has been a most important change in the currency, not only of the United States, but of the world. The volume has been greatly enlarged, not merely by the introduction of a vast quantity of gold, but by the extension of the mixed currency system, through countries where it did not before exist. The consequence has been a great rise in the prices of commodities in general, as well as wages; though the latter have advanced much less in proportion than the former, the laborer receiving a larger sum in currency, but a less share of value than he did before. So great has been the change of prices within the period named, than an exact comparison between the real wages of labor before 1840 and since cannot be made.

There is, therefore, no sufficient evidence that wages have risen in consequence of, or cotemporaneously with, the reduction in the hours of labor.

We here pass to the consideration of a fact quite essential to the discussion of the question of the hours of labor:

The Unity of Labor.

The labor of the world is a unit. Once it was not so.

> "Nations separated by a narrow frith abhorred each other,
> Mountains interposed made enemies of nations."

But such is the case no longer, so far as the interests of industry are concerned. The populations of the earth form one grand brotherhood, bound together by a common destiny. If the conditions or rewards of labor are better in one country than another, the favored country will at once receive contributions of muscle and sinew from all others. The facilities for locomotion in the last half of the nineteenth century are such that it requires but a few days' time, and a few dollars in expense, to transport a full grown laborer from one hemisphere to the other.

The condition of the laborer is now better, his reward greater, in the United States, than in any other quarter of the globe; consequently Europe is pouring in upon us her emigrants from the East, and China from the West. At the late international congress of laboring men at Paris, the fact was referred to, that whenever wages advanced in London, Germans went over by thousands to supply the demand, and this kept down the rate, and that this was the case throughout Europe, owing to the diffusion of intelligence and conveniences for travel. By some this was spoken of as a matter of regret, but such is a mistaken view of the subject. This unity of labor is for the general advantage of all mankind. To regret it, is like regretting the discovery of labor-saving machinery, which throws hand-labor out of immediate employment, but benefits ultimately every human being. This great fact being well established, we see at once that anything which goes to improve the conditions of the laborer, or raise his wages in this country will of a certainty increase immigration, and this will increase the competition for wages. We must not ignore this very important consideration, because it is entirely essential to a correct understanding of the case before us. The question of the hours of labor is the same in its nature as that of wages, and wages are and must be governed by the laws of trade, and those laws are above all human enactments.

If the legislature of Massachusetts could by a mere law limit a day's work to eight hours, and at the same time insure the same wages as when ten hours constituted a day's work, would not the undoubted effect be to increase the competition for employment in this favored State, until the wages were reduced to a point nearly or quite equal to the reduction in the time of service? If so, is it practicable to effect the desired object of reducing the hours of labor, and at the same time insuring equal wages as before?

Govermental Interference.

In regard to all govermental interference in the hours of labor, our conclusion is, that since no one is compelled by law to work, there is no good reason why any one should be forbidden to work,—that government has no rightful control over the labor of free men, who must dispose of their services at all times, in such quantities, and at such rates as they can get, in the great competition of industrial pursuits,—that government can no more in justice or propriety ordain that eight hours shall constitute a day's work, than that eighty cents shall be a dollar, —that all attempts to interfere with the laws of value must be ineffectual for any good object,—that the laborer can never be oppressed by being left at perfect liberty to work as he pleases, —that he is never injured by *competition*, unless the laws or customs of the country deprive him of his just rights. The laborer in our own country to some extent, and in foreign countries to a greater extent, is wronged by social institutions. Especially is the American laborer robbed, at the present time, by a *false currency*, which takes from him nearly or quite one-fourth of what he earns from day to day. Such evils must be endured until the intelligence of the community is sufficient to discover and put an end to them. Let labor be measured by an exact and invariable standard of time, and a sound standard of currency, and the laborer has no occasion to fear that a just compensation will not be secured to him.

Proposed Reduction not Demanded by the People.

From all the observations which the undersigned have been able to make, we are quite satisfied that there is no general sentiment in the Commonwealth in favor of such a measure as the reduction of all the mechanical labor of the country from ten to eight hours. Even amongst the mechanics themselves, we do not think that the proposed measure is looked upon as feasible and desirable. Not that men would not greatly prefer to work eight hours instead of ten each day, if by doing so they could get the same reward ; but we think there is a general conviction that such a thing is impracticable, that it would arrest to an injurious extent the industry of the country, and reduce the general production to such a degree as to greatly restrict the enjoyments of all classes.

There seems to be no enthusiasm in any quarter in behalf of such a reduction. The absence of effective organizations on the subject seems to indicate an intelligent consciousness that the measure is one that cannot, and in reality ought not to be carried.

Gradual Reduction.

Again, if it were decided notwithstanding, that the reduction should be made, the question would still remain whether it should not be a gradual one, made by instalments. So great a change has never yet been attempted at once. The reduction in the hours of factory labor from thirteen to eleven hours was gradually accomplished in a series of some thirty or forty years. It did not take place instantly and universally, but gradually and partially at different times and places, until it is now nearly complete. Yet the reduction from thirteen to eleven hours was but a trifle over fifteen per cent., while the change contemplated as already stated is twenty per cent., or nearly one-third greater. Besides we must remember that in the case of factory operatives, the great majority are females and minors, while in regard to mechanics, all are male adults.

Again, the reduction to ten hours which has come into practice within the last forty years has been, we are assured, rather a systematic arrangement of labor than a reduction of time. Previously there were no established hours; a day's work depended much on the circumstances under which it was performed, and the time of the year in which it was made. There was great irregularity and variation in regard to the whole matter of hours and meals. But the adoption of a ten-hour rule, though it did not essentially lessen the aggregate hours of labor, so systematized them, that both parties, the employer and employed, were benefited by it. The change was effected by the natural progress of industry, not by govermental action. All future changes will doubtless be in the same direction, and we believe will eventually go much farther than is now generally anticipated. As mind triumphs over matter, the necessity for muscular efforts to secure equal results, is constantly diminishing, though it can never wholly disappear.

The natural tendency of things will undoubtedly be in the future as in the past, to a gradual reduction of the hours of labor, and to a continual amelioration of the condition of the laborer. The great inventions and improvements in labor-saving instrumentalities which are constantly increasing the power of labor in production, are rendering it more and more feasible to dispense with a great share of what was once indispensable to human welfare. Perhaps the time has already come when, if there was a general concert of action throughout the world, the hours of labor might be universally reduced, and yet the improvement and civilization of the race go forward. To be sure, there would be a less production of wealth, less for the laborer, and all other classes to enjoy; but, if all were content with this, human happiness and welfare might perhaps be advanced by it. There would be more time for recreation, for reading, for travelling, for mental and moral culture. But to be fully successful, it must be a general, not a partial movement.

Alleged Tyranny of Capital.

A great deal is said in this connection of the "tyranny of capital." But capital has no more power in itself to tyrannize over labor, than labor has to tyrannize over capital,—except that capital can be more readily concentrated and brought to act in masses, and may be said to have more leisure and more opportunity to exert influence on legislation. It has a power more readily wielded than labor. What labor needs to counteract all this, is a greater concentration of its own energies by voluntary associations, and by the diffusion of intelligence, *and that kind of knowledge which appertains to its own interests.* Nothing promises so much for the advantage of workingmen as these associated efforts for useful purposes, for the promotion of good morals and the protection of the defenceless. By union and co-operation, not only may all their rights be secured, but they may largely participate in the profits of trade and manufacture.

This, we know, they are already doing with almost incredible success in Europe, and to some extent in this country; and if regardful of their own interests, they will extend these efforts as far and as widely as possible. Capital has more *independence* than labor, that is, it is not compelled as labor often is, to act under unfavorable circumstances. It should always, therefore, be an object of the first importance in the mind of the laborer, to secure a certain degree of *independence* himself, by practising such frugality as to lay by so much of his earnings as will prevent the necessity of working *at once*, whether he can get reasonable terms or not. This we regard as a matter of the first importance to the laboring classes. Accumulations, however limited, promote not only the self-respect and independence of those who make them, but the respect and confidence of those who employ them. The amount of deposits in savings banks, so far as made by the working classes, forms *the best index* of the real progress of those classes, in pecuniary independence and in social improvement.

Circulars to Workingmen.

At this point we take leave to insert the circular before alluded to, sent to those who were supposed especially to represent the interests of labor:—

Boston, October 3, 1866.

Dear Sir:—As a citizen of Massachusetts, you are presumed to be interested in the present investigation of the subject of the Hours of Labor; "*especially in its relations to the social, educational and sanitary condition of the industrial classes, and to the permanent prosperity of the productive industry of the State.*" Will you be so kind as to give as brief answers, by letter, as are consistent to the following queries, or to any portion of them?

1. In what manner would a reduction of daily labor, to Eight Hours, affect you socially, by its influence on you in moral, political or domestic duties and privileges?
2. What would be the effect of reduced hours on mental development?
3. State the length of your day's work; also the time and distance you travel, and the time required in domestic duties.
4. Was any deduction made in the wages of labor when the ten-hour system was introduced?
5. Was the reduction in time made at once, or by successive steps?
6. Has the custom of ten hours of actual labor been shortened by the introduction of railroads?
7. What is the effect of the hours of labor on the choice of a place of residence?

Answers to these inquiries are requested, if possible, before the first of November.

Amasa Walker,
William Hyde,
Edward H. Rogers,
Commissioners.

To about four hundred and fifty of these circulars sent out, some forty replies were received, as a general fact, earnestly in favor of a reduction from ten to eight hours for mechanical labor. We insert three of these letters, quite different in their general tone, but representing, no doubt, to a fair extent, the average sentiment of that class to whom the circulars were addressed.

[Letter No. 1.]

To the Commissioners of the Hours of Labor.

GENTLEMEN :—In answer to the questions proposed in your circular, in relation to shortening the hours of daily labor, I would say,—

1st. That a reduction of the term of labor to *ten hours* per day, would give to the operative classes more time for the cultivation of those fraternal sympathies by which human beings are united together in associative bonds. It would promote the moral improvement of the masses, by bringing them up to the standard of better and more enlightened society. It would cause them to value more highly, and seek more earnestly, the acquisition of political knowledge, and afford them more time for the study thereof. It would secure better order in the domestic circles of the working classes for similar reasons.

2d. A reduction in the hours of labor would improve the mental condition of the operatives, by raising them to a state of illumination, which they could not, (in the very nature of things,) otherwise attain. I fearlessly aver, that this statement is fully sustained in the history and experience of the past few years.

3d. The length of a day's work in our factories is from eleven to eleven and a quarter hours. A considerable portion of the mill operatives of Lowell, reside from half a mile to one mile from their work. It requires from twenty minutes to half an hour to walk the respective distances,—the distances are from one to two miles, calculating both ways. We have forty-five minutes allowed for dinner; and if we deduct from twenty minutes to half an hour from forty-five, it only leaves fifteen minutes for one class, and twenty-five for the other, to eat dinner and perform the domestic duties. We swallow our food in a partially masticated state, thereby occasioning dyspepsia and other distressing symptoms.

4th. I am not aware of one single instance where any deduction was made in wages of the operative when the *ten-hour system* was introduced ; but I do know, that wages have advanced about twenty-five per cent. since the enactment of the ten-hour law.*

5th. The reduction of time was made at once.

6th. I am not prepared to say, what the precise influence of the introduction of railroads has in shortening the hours of labor.

* There has never been any such law.—*Commissioners.*

7th. Working classes have virtually no choice in a place of residence, but are necessitated to take up with the most miserable accommodations.

Yours, for   LABOR REFORM.

NOTE.—I have confined my remarks to the ten-hour system, as I believe it to be the only practicable standard which we are likely to obtain from our corporation friends, and seems to me to be the most reasonable.

[Letter No. 2.]

GENTLEMEN :—Your circular came to hand the 22d ; I take the earliest opportunity of replying to those "queries" to the best of my personal knowledge.

To query 1. I think if the hours of labor were reduced to eight I should be more social in my own family. Through the summer months I return from my labors weary in mind and body; my better nature and good nature are pretty well ground down, and I am not the pleasant husband and father my natural disposition inclines me to be. Mirthfulness and good nature don't go hand in hand with over-work. I think we should be better neighbors ; it would give us time to visit and be sociable, to indulge in social amusements, keep up our youth and not become old men at forty-five. I think it would tend to make me a more constant church-goer. I should not feel compelled to make the Sabbath a day for bodily rest, and a good sermon would make double the impression upon a mind free from weariness. The Sunday's sermon now comes at the end of a hard six days' work. I have a bathing apparatus but seldom make use of it, for weariness at night and lack of time in the morning; so this great promoter of health is lost to us through the very season we most need it.

I am satisfied I make many losses each year by making purchases by lamplight ; get deceived in quality of goods or other articles that daylight would show its defects. If we are unfortunate enough before marrying and having a family dependent upon us, to acquire any accomplishment, as music &c., it must be abandoned ; we must slide into ignorance and barbarism ; we cannot do without *work*, but every darling accomplishment that lifts us over the stony paths of life, we must leave to mourn over the balance of our lives. The want of more time at home, the weariness of the mind and body and tired nature's ever recurring demand for sleep, are the great enemies of men of constant toil. * * *

[Letter No. 3.]

MR. CHAIRMAN—*Sir:*—Having your circular before me I will answer your questions in the order named.

1st. I do not think it would be of much value to me, from the fact that I now have from three to five hours daily for domestic duties, reading, attending lectures, &c., which is enough for a man who has a family to support, and who desires a small balance in bank for a "wet day."

2d. The answers to the first would cover the second.

3d. I get up regularly winter and summer (Sundays excepted) at 5½ o'clock, and leave at 7 for ——, returning at 6½ P. M. to my house, giving about nine hours working time and two hours in the journey. I spend less than one hour per day in domestic duties.

4th. "Was any deduction made in the wages of labor when the ten-hour system was introduced?" No, from the fact that as much is now performed as was under the old system. Labor was immediately reduced to a system of beginning on time,—no leaving off for meals and a closer application to business. A further reduction would be impossible to obtain the same amount of work, without injury to the body.

5th. I think it was adopted at once as regards mechanical work.

6th. I think it may,—it has in my case.

7th. It has no effect with me.

Now Mr. Chairman, allow me briefly to offer some suggestions as they appear to me.

The eight-hour agitation seems unnecessary to me, but it may lead to *piece*, or *contract work*, or *association work*. Simply an eight-hour law, without a compulsatory clause compelling capital to hire at such prices and at such times as would suit the employed, would be of no value to labor; capital would adjust itself to the new order of things. I have lived upwards of fifty years and have never yet found the person who was willing to accept eighty cents for one hundred, and never expect to. This movement starts with the gross assumption that none have rights but the employed. It is nowhere proposed to reduce the pay in the same ratio, but "pass the law and we will compel capital to grant us the terms." The whole affair from the beginning is an outrage on common sense, and fair dealing between man and man. The demand for a law is unnecessary, because we all, or most of the laboring people can make an arrangement now with their employer to work eight, nine or more hours, if circumstances make it desirable. I have always been able to do so, and will never surrender that right without a struggle.

Again, its enactment would be a gross insult and a standing evidence of the degradation of the laboring classes. It would be virtually saying to them, that they were incapable of making their own contracts.

Taking my own case and looking over the vast range of circumstances and conditions that go to modify the various occupations of men, such as climate, physical and mechanical ability, in-door and out-door work, unwholesome and dangerous trades, &c., &c., it seems impossible that any one can seriously propose it.

To me it would be as absurd as to ask of the legislature to pass a law declaring that every person should eat, drink, and sleep the same time, and wear the same coat.

The rights of American citizens are the same, be they bosses, capitalists or laborers—each performs its part, and all are necessary to the great whole, and any attempt to ignore or deny to either party those rights, will be resisted.

I now pass to another point that will, if adopted, settle this question forever; namely, piece-work. In fact I can see no possible objection to it, except by those who expect to receive service or pay for which they do not give an equivalent; and above all, let the same price be allowed for the same work, whether it be performed by male or female hands. Piece-work is the only true, just and dignified arrangement to both parties—it has less of the overseerism about it and objectionable features, to disturb a sensitive mind—besides, judging by my intercourse with those trades-people that have adopted piece-work, and those that have not, I find the former more intelligent and cheerful, have more manly and womanly dignity and self-respect, and take a higher social and intellectual position, than those that work on time. And last though not least, associative efforts. Why not? Is it more difficult for twenty carpenters to join together for the pursuit of their business than for a like number of musicians? We have the latter in our midst in perfect success. Let the several trades have a place of business, with an agent responsible to them, and the community, and then they will be in a fair way to reap the entire benefits of their labor.

Hoping that whatever else may happen, the time may never come when the intelligent American people are to be considered unable to make their own bargains either concerning the number of hours that shall constitute a day's work, or the price thereof, I submit the questions to the serious consideration of your committee, whose efforts are for the good of the human race.

We might give more of these expressions of opinion by the workingmen and women of Massachusetts, but our limits forbid further extracts.

The Example of Massachusetts.

It has been maintained by some, that although it may be impracticable to fix the hours of labor for the various branches of industry in the country, it is expedient that the legislature of this State should enact that eight hours shall be a day's work for all mechanics in its own employ. The argument in favor of this measure is, that the *moral effect* of such action on the part of the government will tend to establish eight hours as the limit of a day's work everywhere. The question in relation to this proposal is, whether the State wishes to give its sanction to the *principle*, that eight hours is the true limit of a day's work, to which all the industry of the State ought to conform? If so, then the law proposed may well be adopted. If, on the the other hand, the legislature of the Commonwealth is not satisfied that eight hours should be the legal day's work anywhere and everywhere, it ought to set *no such example;* it should exert no such moral influence.

We believe the time has come when the hours of labor in some of the severer trades should be reduced from ten hours to a less number. The work may be gradually accomplished, if thought best. Every half hour deducted from the toil of those who are called by the severity of their employment to exert to the utmost every faculty of mind and body, would be a great benefaction. Then, again, not only are some trades much more severe and exhaustive than others, but the seasons of the year greatly influence the condition of the laborer. In winter the days are short and inclement; and to be compelled, as many are, to rise at five o'clock, and be off to work at six, in the dark and cold, is undoubtedly a hardship from which any one may well be desirous to be released. It would seem, therefore, that a reduction of hours in certain trades, especially in the winter season, ought to be effected, not by law, but by a public sentiment which would induce the employer to make the change.

THE HOUR AS A MEASURE OF LABOR.

It is proposed in some quarters that a general law be enacted *in the absence of any contract*, that the legal day's work shall be eight hours. The consequence of such an enactment would be to compel the adoption of a general contract system by the hour, instead of the day. In so far, the result would be a highly favorable one. All work should be measured by *the hour*. It is the only proper unit of time in relation to labor. It is a definite and invariable quantity, which all understand; while *a day*, as a measure of labor, is a variable and undefined space of time, in regard to which there must be a constant opportunity for disagreement and dissatisfaction. In agriculture, in olden times, *a day* meant from sun to sun, except in haying time, and then it meant from daylight in the morning until the hay was duly secured at night ; but in the present state of things in this country, a day's work has no definite limit whatever. It would be a wise arrangement, on the part of all engaged in business, if their contracts for labor were made entirely by the hour instead of the day, and from present appearances such can hardly fail to be the final result. It would settle all questions of dispute in regard to the hours of labor, as each person would agree to work as many hours as he pleased, and be content to fulfil his contract, whatever it might be. It may be a matter of question whether it would not be good policy to enact that no contracts for labor not made upon the hour standard should be recognized in law.

In view of the foregoing considerations, the undersigned would respectfully represent to your Excellency, that they cannot recommend the enactment of any law restricting the hours of labor for the adult population of the Commonwealth, but in accordance with what has already been observed, they would suggest that if there be any persons unconvicted of crime in the employ of the State, whose duties are of an especially laborious and exhaustive character, that the hours of labor for such persons should, under the direction of the Executive, be reduced to such an extent as humanity and the nature of the case may seem to require.

AMASA WALKER.
WILLIAM HYDE.

To His Excellency ALEXANDER H. BULLOCK, *Governor of Massachusetts.*

The undersigned, as Commissioner on the Hours of Labor, has the honor to present the following

MINORITY REPORT:

The relations between capital and labor are not as yet so well adjusted as to preclude an attentive hearing in an issue like the present to both interests. It has been truly said, that " reductions in hours are to so great an extent laborers' questions, that the feelings of the people themselves are of the most primary importance in forming a judgment." A generous appreciation on the part of your Excellency of the interests of labor in this respect has given me an opportunity of presenting its present condition and tendencies, in connection with principles which, it is confidently believed, are destined to exert a weighty influence on the future of our country.

The means at my disposal to do this, are derived from intimate, personal and traditional knowledge of the condition and progress of mechanical labor in this State ; notes taken at the hearings before the Legislative Committee of 1865 ; the phonographic reports of testimony before, and the letters sent to, the first Commission ; several public hearings before the present Commission, with correspondence, examination of the Parliamentary debates on the Factory Bill, and other public documents and papers, including twenty-five valuable pamphlets, kindly forwarded by the Rev. Charles Hill, Secretary of the Workingman's Lord's Day Rest Association, 13 Bedford Row, London.

The attendance of workingmen at the advertised hearings of the present Commission has been so scanty as to give rise to inquiry for the cause. Three series of hearings in succession, during eighteen months, had been improved by the authorized representatives of the organizations of labor; their views were on record in the documents already referred to, and were, by common consent, deemed sufficient under the circumstances.

A similar inquiry may with propriety be made for the reasons why so few responses have been returned to the citizens' circular. They are to be found in the fact, that the daily habits of our people are so exclusively laborious as to unfit them for giving a ready expression to thought. That this is consistent with high intelligence and respectability may be seen by the admissions in the agricultural reports of the present situation of the farming interest in reference to accounts, diaries, and correspondence.

Some circumstances personal to myself seem to render it proper for me to state a few of the reasons for uniting with my associates in the measures they propose in reference to factory labor. Up to the moment of accepting a place on the Commission, I held no matured views on the hours of labor of the farms and mills, simply believing that decided reductions in both were required for the good of society. My views in this respect were expressed in a letter to the first Commission, an imperfect abstract of which appears on page sixty-five of their report. In harmony with the sentiment which I have quoted at the beginning of these remarks I am free to say that I have no theoretic views on this subject which I should attempt to urge, in advance of the expressed wish of those most interested,—the laboring classes themselves. A thorough search of the recorded testimony, and diligent inquiry throughout the State, wherever I have been, has failed to discover to me the first mill operative in favor of any present reduction below ten hours. Under these circumstances, I should have felt culpable in withholding my assent from the conclusions of the majority of the Commission.

At the same time, I desire to place myself on record, as disbelieving that there is any necessity, which cannot ultimately be removed, for the continuance of so long a term of labor for females and children as sixty hours per week, in such unhealthy conditions. While recognizing cheerfully the praiseworthy efforts made in some localities to relieve the factory system of its worst exposures, the conviction is still strong upon me that, in some of its features, it is obviously at variance with sound commercial laws and those high moralities towards which, by the results of our institutions of religion, government and education, we are tending.

I have approached with careful consideration the question of the labor of the farms; though not familiar personally with its details, I realize some of the burdens under which it is carried on; but with all due allowance for them, the position taken by the farming interest seems to me to be vulnerable. The sturdy opposition of the class of small employers, foremen, &c., to the reduction of hours in the trades, was as marked in its character as that which is now heard from the country, but it has been silenced by experience, and many are now willing witnesses to the truths which formerly they opposed. Items of direct pecuniary gain, in connection with reduction, are well known to workmen of this experience, and are happily paralleled in an able lecture delivered at the annual meeting of the State Board of Agriculture, at Worcester, page 187 Report of '65 and '66.

" The ways of waste on a farm are great and innumerable, and the farmer made negligent and inattentive by over-labor, by a hasty, slovenly and inadequate method, will stumble upon most of them. A ruinous, leaky, rat-infested barn, pelting lean cattle with cold winds from every quarter, will, with one stroke of loss, reduce profits by half.

" The mechanic would be utterly ruined by a negligence familiar to many, if not most, farmers."

The central truth, in its economic relations, of the first reduction, seems to be that the average laborer will produce as much, to say the least, in a single season in ten hours as in twelve. The reduced hours strike broadly away from drinking habits, and from a generally coarse and wasteful condition of hired labor toward one approximating to a hopeful and thoughtful celerity of effort. The indications in agricultural literature that this is what is needed, are sufficiently obvious to remove all fear for the results of the change, whenever accomplished. I have endeavored to show, in the article on the growth of cities, that the present situation of the hired labor of the farms, in connection with the training of the sons of farmers, has results more disastrous to our social equilibrium. The gravitation of labor and capital to the cities is accelerated by the great advantages of education which the in-comers find for their children. It seems worth consideration, whether appropriations from the school fund could not be so distributed as to equalize these conditions.

Boston, with public schools which are the admiration of the world, is the 315th from the head of the list of the percentage of appropriations for their support; while the farming towns are burdened with much higher rates, with results so inadequate as in many cases to appear simply as a burlesque on any proper view of what schools should be.

In the ten articles which I present to your Excellency as embodying the ideas to which I have been led in this inquiry, I have endeavored, by illustration and argument, to bring prominently to view three truths of sufficient moment to affect powerfully national development. These are,

First. The doctrine of Channing, that "MANUAL LABOR IS THE DIVINE TRAINING TO ENERGIZE THE CHARACTER."

Second. That of Ellesmere, "THE MORE HOURS MEN WORK IN ANY STAPLE BRANCH OF MANUFACTURES THE LESS THEY RECEIVE IN THE FORM OF WAGES;" and

Third. The view that LABOR IS CAPITAL.

Beginning with an historic sketch of the progress of the reform of labor in Massachusetts, I pass to a statement of the causes and connection of the eight hour movement, first developing Channing's view of the tendencies of manual labor. Alluding freely as I have to the fact, that the reduction already partially accomplished is, by the daily exercise of one of the most extraordinary elements in human affairs, that of sacrifice, it costs me nothing to admit that in its introduction and adjustment a further abbreviation of working time will involve an *apparent* loss. That this will not be in amount anything like the fifteen per cent. on the whole production of the country, usually claimed by those opposing, will be seen by noting the slow progress of the ten hour movement, thus proving that its adoption will be gradual, allowing ample time for the compensations which will result, to ingraft themselves upon every interest of society. If this sacrifice referred solely to the labor of animals, close observation, in connection with experience, might enable us to gauge by figures the merits of the change ; but applying as it does to the boundless capacities of human beings, and liberating forces as powerful and instantaneously operative as the closing of the waters under the stern of the advancing ship, it transcends arithmetic calculation. The statistical genius of Halliday would fail in the effort to note the accession of productive power by the attraction to labor of intelligent youth from the middle classes, who, under present conditions become non-producers, or to trace the influx from another class, now fearfully drawn upon by the mortality resulting from idleness and dissipation,—the children of the educated and wealthy. The view which commands the assent of a considerable portion of the industrial community, that it will pay to make the change, even if it does cost something in enhancement of price, seems to be in harmony with those Providential developments by which the race is advanced by sacrifice. We cannot show any increase of ships, or houses, or personal property, sufficient to account fully for the recent inflation in our valuations, but we have thrown off a moral incubus which laid like lead upon the heart of the nation ; we feel that our property is worth more in consequence, and we believe in an unbounded advance in material prosperity, because we have thus relieved ourselves of a foul abomination. First righteous, then prosperous, has been uttered by one who enters by divine right into the arrangements of all human economies ; the question is not whether the operative at the loom or the machinist at the lathe can produce as much to-day, in eight hours, as they did yesterday in ten ; *but what is the use which the Divine Being intended should be made of the incarnation of his own creative powers in modern inventions.*

The need of week-day, as well as Sabbath, leisure, is indicated with impressive significance in the only legislation which has come to us with the special stamp of divine authority. The intimate association of the command alluded to in the sixth article, with the foundation truths of morality, seems sufficient proof of the necessity for a general application of the principle involved.

Shall the great accessions of productive power be allowed to flow in the channels of commercial law, not only unimpeded, but aided by legislation and all the prestige of social influence ?

If, from whatever cause, we assent to this, we have prophetic indications of the unavoidable results of such local and individual centralization of wealth, in the gloomy tragedies which convulse our cities. Our institutions of religion and education will fail to relieve us, until their power is brought to bear directly on our industrial system; free schools and free churches will struggle with but partial success against the power of daily influences. Let us give full force to them, and to our noble Northern sentiment of honor to labor, by distinctive recognition of its injurious results with the present hours; and put the crown upon American civilization by practical acknowledgment of the fact that human labor cannot with impunity be lowered to the level of its own material results. The argument of the two articles next succeeding, Social Elevation and Instruction in Labor, is in the direction of remuneration for sacrifice.

The fifth article, the relation of the hours of labor to the farm, has been incidentally alluded to.

The question of the moral condition and tendencies of the masses, in the sixth article, is argued under the disadvantage of silence as to similar exposures on the part of the influential portion of society. When the most ignorant and bigoted portion of the people of our neighboring countries are massed together in our towns without any of that thoughtful consideration which is so pleasingly evident in a portion of our large manufacturing cities, and in some of the small ones, the question presents itself to every candid mind, whether the moral condition of the one can be considered without a glance at the other.

It is a very grateful duty to me to give publicity to the fact, that there is a spirit pervading the State in favor of reform. I have heard many earnest expressions, accompanied with deeds, in the direction of a better condition of labor than has hitherto existed.

Unless the best mind of England is theoretically and practically at fault, reductions in hours would elevate the masses by tending to a better observance of the Sabbath.

The influences now operating adversely, are not only tacit and habitual, but they are aided by a very respectable, but as I think, mistaken, portion of our labor reformers. The following argument, from an English source, against secularization, is not without its applicability to ourselves:—

"Workingmen, for your own sakes and your children's, consider and weigh well the serious and terrible consequences with which this scheme is fraught. You cannot be ignorant of the national character of the English. Instead of the hilarity and comparative freedom from the pride of wealth which appear in other countries, and which *might* preserve the Sunday as a mere holiday, the steady, persevering, commercial bias of Englishmen would soon turn it into a working day. Among ourselves, the pushing of trade in brisk times, the fierceness of competition, and the eagerness to secure wealth, would soon trench upon the leisure of a mere secular day, and would, without thinking it did you wrong, make it one of productive labor. Even now, the money-making spirit of England exacts excessive toil from the working classes; but how much more would this be the case if the scriptural command that claims the Sabbath for rest were broken down. Would a manufacturer who had a pressing order to execute, be kept from demanding work on the Sunday by being told it was the day for amusement? Would a tradesman who saw his neighbor's shop open, keep his closed if he were persuaded that the Sabbath was no longer a day of divine obligation? Would a farmer, morbidly afraid of bad weather, be deterred from sending his laborers into the fields, if he believed that the Sunday was no more a religious day than the Wednesday? Those who think so know very little about Englishmen, and are not fit to be the guides of public opinion.

"I lay great stress, and I think justly, on the peculiar temperament of the English nation in this argument. There is among us a conventional sentiment around the possession of wealth, and attached to success in business, which hurries men into such a vortex of temptation as would soon overpower the claim for recreation on the Sabbath. If, then, you sweep away the old religious foundation for the observance of the day, —if there are to be no ramparts around it but mere secular advantages, what help is there for the workingmen? for fences like these would, in our race for riches, be like straws before the whirlwind."

The next, the relations of labor to the growth of cities, draws attention to some points of the utmost importance in our national development. The relation existing between hours and wages, is discussed at sufficient length in connection with its central truth, to relieve me from further allusion.

In the plea for the establishment of a standard of time for labor, I have taken a practical view of its claims for legal recognition. I am unable to see that the argument there presented loses any of its logical value on account of the fact that reductions have been accomplished without such standards being formally recognized. Great nationalities have said, in response to this request, "I go not," but impelled by circumstantial exigencies, while denying the theory, they have practically answered its requirements by official mandates and legislation for minors. With an exception due to the extraordinary power of the trades, as such, in England,—a condition which there is not the slightest prospect of reaching in this country,—I have shown that workmen, or laborers, cannot obliterate alone the deep furrows of habit, in the daily estimate of time; that they are as helpless in this respect as any department of commerce would be in an effort to introduce the metric system without similar aid. Argued to its finer issues, this inquiry takes us to the sources of all human effort; a few yards of silk, used as a military standard, embodies and links together the daily routine of life, with the profoundest emotions which animate the human breast. Without it, soldiery would be soulless mobs, and the deep degradation of the classes of labor most exposed by the breaking down of rules, ought to be a sufficient refutation of the theory that the guiding, monitory influence of legislation, which stops short of adult coercion, is any infringement of a proper individual freedom.

As the last of my points of inquiry, I briefly notice the ideas which cluster around the question of labor, as seen from its highest aspects.

I have reached the conclusion indicated on this point, after a thorough consideration of the influences which, in these days, are tending to a more direct recognition of immaterial forces in connection with productive results.

Definitions of capital, which confine it to accumulated products of a visible character, seem to me inadequate. The exclusion of the moral, intellectual, ideal, and energizing forces by economists, from their idea of wealth, I regard as fatal to the comprehensiveness of their views. The meaning of venerable formulas in religious doctrine, and of long-received commercial axioms, have been drifted out of the words in which they are couched, solely because their sharply-defined literalism has proved inadequate to retain within their grasp advancing knowledge. In my estimate of the value of the cotton produced in the South the past season, I cannot distinguish—in their relation to productiveness—between the personal qualities furnished by the laborer and the appliances supplied by capital; the present status and productive power of the freedmen, is as directly the result of self-control as a Northern cotton gin is of the economic virtues of the section from which it came. To consider the last as capital, and to ignore, or to assign to other departments of human interest, the accumulated results of brain labor, under the agonizing tuition of slavery, will hardly bear our present intellectual tests, or meet the strain of social and national exigencies. To admit that "the poor man's labor is his only capital," in some of its aspects leads us to the verge of the principle contended for, but in others it falls far short of truth. When we remember that what is sentient nerve in the laborer's palm, a few feet higher up expands without a break into a substance allying by its functions its possessor to Divinity, a reasonable doubt may be raised whether the axiom is of sufficient value to use in any but the most common-place connections.

The fact that human labor does not advance in its price to the point reached by commodities, is admitted. The reason for this, as explained in the light of the enlarged views of the distinguished citizen, under whom I have the honor of serving on this Commission, I accept. " Human labor is so connected with personality, as to be beyond the control of its possessor, or any other party, for hoarding with speculative views." It cannot be bought up and held for a rise in the manner in which merchandise is; so that, in fact, it tends to remain as to its price, or what is the same thing, the income of its possessor, on the same plane of value that merchandise would, if, by the general adoption of the co-operative principle, the function of commerce was simply to forward to the consumer.

This, it is evident to me it will do, as long as it is considered solely as a commodity. The grandeur of man is thus seen to be closely connected with those depressing circumstances, which have favored, and almost forced skepticism, as to the practicability of a comprehensive elevation of the masses; but if these views are founded in truth, the interests of industry will find their greatest strength in their weakest point, and the truth of the axiom that extremes meet, will reach its grandest and most beneficent illustration.

I conclude this introduction with drawing the attention of your Excellency to the fact, that over a great portion of the globe, the equatorial belt, a day of labor shorter than that in use for the farm and factory employ of our State, is enforced by the darkness which immediately succeeds the setting of the sun in tropical regions, and the exposure to venomous and sanguinary animals which ensues, thus forcing the laborer to reach his home by the light. And also, that the religious observances of a large majority of the populations of the temperate portions of the earth sensibly relieve them, in addition to the Sabbath, from continuous toil. It will be noticed in the Report, that the heavy trades of England are in advance of us in the case of the masons and joiners, to which may be added the shipbuilders of the Clyde, after a protracted contest the past season. The English workmen, with but a moiety of our weighty responsibilities resting upon them, have indicated in the most decisive manner that their competition shall not hinder us from desirable results.

For figures bearing with much emphasis on our intense Massachusetts life, I refer you to page seventy-three of the twenty-third Registration Report, where it appears that out of 26,717 drafted men, 14,181, or 530+ in every thousand, were exempted for disability; the proportion in Maine being 415; in New Hampshire, 344; New York, 306; and also state, that an analysis of the United States Census for 1860, which appears not to have been refuted, gives the yearly deaths in our State, as one in fifty-seven,—there being but one State in the Union more unhealty,—Arkansas having one death in every forty-eight of her population.

Historic Sketch of Labor Reform in Massachusetts.

It is difficult to trace the origin and course of the movement for the first reduction of the hours of labor. It did not obtain a free expression through the press. I have not seen the term "ten hours" in the established journalism of the country during the period of its agitation. This, however, excites less surprise, from the fact that the advocates of reform often omit reference to the duration of labor. An occasional allusion shows that workingmen were organized, in some cases as will be seen, uniting with the farming interest.*

January 21, 1834, the first meeting for the formation of a union of trades, was held at the Old Common Council Room, Court Square, Boston, and a committee appointed to take such measures as they should deem expedient, to effect the formation of a general trades' union of the mechanics of Boston and vicinity; the committee thus appointed met at Bascom's hotel, School Street, on the evening of January 28. The several trades were generally represented in the committee. They issued a circular proposing a plan, which was responded to by sixteen branches of labor. They met the first Tuesday in March and adopted a constitution, which was subsequently ratified by the different trades. Under the auspices of this union, a procession, oration and dinner, were arranged and carried into execution on the Fourth of July, 1834. There were said to have been about two thousand men in the procession.

The following card appeared as an advertisement in the "Morning Post" of July 8:—

"The Committee of Arrangements for the Trades' Union Celebration of the Fourth of July, return their sincere thanks to the various individuals and societies who have so kindly countenanced and assisted them in their endeavors to show a proper regard to the birth-day of their country.

"To the Shipwrights of Charlestown, for their great exertions in contributing so largely to the splendor and appearance of the occasion, (by furnishing a ship.)

"To Mr. Wentworth, and those who assisted him, for the generous aid afforded in drawing the vessel, and to the officers and crew who so skilfully navigated her.

---

* I find the first evidence of this in some manuscripts, furnished me too late in my inquiry to receive the notice they deserve. From them I learn that a convention of delegates from the farmers, mechanics, and workingmen of New England, was held in the Representatives' Hall of the State House at Boston, in September, 1832. Grievances were discussed, and resolutions and an address adopted, setting forth the burdens under which the laboring classes suffered from excessive hours, imprisonment for debt, the lack of a lien law, onerous militia service, and various other causes.

"To Capt. Snelling, and the company under his command, for their prompt and vigorous escort.

"To the proprietors of the Federal Street Theatre, for the use of their furniture.

"To the Commandant of the Navy Yard, for the use of decorations.

"To the North End Artillery, for their grand salute.

"To those whose decorations of the streets through which we passed evinced a spirit of co-operation with us.

"To the Reader of the Declaration of Independence, and of the Bill of Rights, for the excellent and appropriate manner in which he performed that service.

"To the Toast-master, for the impartial and excellent discharge of his duty.

"To such editors as have made favorable notices of our proceedings, especially the Editor of the 'Evening Gazette,' who voluntarily published our transactions of the day.

"To the citizens who, by their attendance to hear the oration and the cheering, and evident gratification with which they greeted our progress, gave evidence of their good feeling toward us.

"To each and all, the Committee return their sincere acknowledgments, and, trusting in the purity of their motives, the goodness of their cause and the importance of their objects, feel assured they will never regret extending toward us the favor we thus publicly acknowledge.

"By order of the Committee of Arrangements of the Trades' Union.

B. H. HAMMATT."

From a pamphlet containing the oration of Frederick Robinson, Esq., in the library of the Athenæum, I take the following notes, indicative of the condition and prospects of labor at that time :—

"It behooves us to ask ourselves, what we have done for the dissemination of a just knowledge of their own rights, among the great mass of the people."

"The immediate interests of the thousands, are always contrary to the interests of the millions."

"When men enter into a state of society, all those rights which it is impossible to enjoy without the aid of others, become social rights, and must be enjoyed, if at all, by concert with others."

"The cause of the people, I trust and believe, is now advancing. And it only needs for us to carry the first, the great reform which we have proposed,—the equal, mental and physical education of all—and our emancipation from the power of aristocracy, will be effective."

"We are yet but a half-educated and half-civilized people. The few are educated in one-half of their faculties, and the people in the other half. The many have been obliged to devote their whole time to bodily labor, while the powers of the mind have been almost entirely neglected."

Of American society he says, " the millions have been lulled into a fatal security, while the thousands have been active in promoting their own interests."

In the course of his remarks, he alludes forcibly to the usurpations of the judiciary, and calls for legislative interference with the hours in factories.

The oration was delivered in the open air on Fort Hill, after which the procession marched to Faneuil Hall. When the company were seated, the following remarks were made:—

" Gentlemen,—The Committee of Arrangements have an apology to make to their fellow-citizens. They regret to say, that no one of our respected clergy are present,—application having been made to twenty-two different religious societies, for the use of a meeting-house on this day for the Trades' Union,—the doors of all were shut against us, and, under the circumstances, your Committee felt a delicacy in applying to any clergyman to officiate at the table, lest he might consider it an affront. We hope that this statement will be deemed a sufficient apology for the deficiency, and that we may all, nevertheless, partake of the bounties spread before us with grateful hearts."

From a long list of toasts, I select two of the most practical:—

" Our brethren at New York—They have struck the first blow at oppression; may success attend, and prosperity crown, all their lawful undertakings."

" Manual Labor Schools—The salvation of our institutions, and the hope of the children of the poor."

Literary History of Labor Reform.

The earliest indication which I find that the movement had attracted the attention of refined circles, is a lecture by Edward Everett, before the Charlestown Lyceum, October 6th, 1830. The impression left upon the mind by its reading is favorable, so far as its liberality is concerned. Broadly interpreted, the following extract seems prophetic of our recent national experience:—

"I will observe, in the first place, then, that if, as I have endeavored to show, man is by nature a working being, it would follow that a workingmen's party is founded in the very principles of our nature. Most parties may be considered as artificial in their very essence. Many are local, temporary and personal. What will all our political parties be a hundred years hence? What are they now, in nine-tenths of the habitable globe? Mere nonentities.

"But the workingmen's party, however organized, must subsist in every civilized country to the end of time. In other words, its first principles are laid in our nature."

The principal defect of the lecture lies in its assertion of the practical identity of mental and physical labor, as is shown by the following language, used after an allusion to callings of the character first named:—

"It needs no words to show that all these pursuits are in reality connected with the ordinary work of society as directly as the mechanical trades by which it is carried on."

November 13, 1831, he speaks again on the same subject before the Franklin Institute, of Boston. There is no direct allusion in either lecture to a reduction of hours. The last, by implication, takes ground against any such change.

During the interval between 1830 and 1840, when the movement of labor culminated in success, I find no writer or speaker of note addressing the public on questions of labor except Channing. Pregnant allusions abound throughout his works, the fullest expression of which is found in his lectures on the elevation of the laboring classes, volume five of his complete works.

On page 159 he lays down this proposition, indicating his views of the design of Providence in placing the human race, to so great an extent, under the necessities of labor:—

"Manual labor is a school in which men are placed to get energy of purpose and character."

The depth of his views on this and kindred subjects is revealed in the assertion that

"The present civilization of the Christian world stands in direct hostility to the great ideas of Christianity."

He defines his relation to the present question in the following words :—

"We do not find that civilization lightens men's toils, as yet it has increased them; and in this I see the sign of a deep defect in what we call the progress of society."

Meanwhile discussion and agitation seem to have been transpiring in magazines and newspapers of an humbler order than those now found on the files of our great libraries. I notice in a periodical of the year 1835, entitled the "Young Mechanic," an able article, headed, "A Plea for the Laboring Classes," written by Mr. George W. Light, on the occasion of the refusal by the authorities of the city of Boston of the use of a hall for an evening meeting, to discuss the ten-hour movement.

He evidently argues against the pressure of a dominant social influence, but very fairly and powerfully; making a strong point against the assumption that the people would abuse time by showing such a doubt to be an arraignment of Divine Providence in granting the race one-seventh of the week.

Political History.

Simultaneously with the developments thus briefly reviewed, political agitation reveals itself in such newspaper items as the following :—

"The Democratic workingmen will celebrate the anniversary of our National Independence at Milford, on the 4th of July next. Entertainment by Col. Sumner. Oration in the brick Meeting-House by Abel Cushing, Esq., of Dorchester."—*Boston Post, June* 24, 1834.

The "Post" of September 3d, 1834, states :—

"On Thursday evening a very full and spirited meeting was held in the old Common Council Room, and ten delegates chosen to the Convention of Farmers, Mechanics and others, to be holden at Northampton on the second Wednesday of September. This meeting was in response to a call to the workingmen of Boston."

The "Boston Mercantile Journal" of June 3, 1835, has an article stating:—

"For two or three years there has been in this State a workingmen's party, who have had candidates for governor, lieutenant-governor, &c."

As the result of the agitation throughout the country, the following memorable Order was issued by President Van Buren. The copy, at present in my possession, was obtained from the Washington Navy Yard by the Hon. Alexander H. Rice, of Boston, and forwarded by him to Mr. J. S. Remick, of Charlestown.

[Extract from General Orders for the regulation of the Navy Yard, Washington, D.C.]

"NAVY YARD, WASHINGTON, April 10, 1840.

"By direction of the President of the United States, 'all public establishments' will hereafter be regulated, as to working hours, by the 'ten-hour system.' The hours for labor in this yard will therefore be as follows, viz.: From the first day of April to the 30th day of September, inclusive, from 6 o'clock, A. M., to 6 o'clock, P. M. During this period, the workmen will breakfast before going to work, for which purpose the bell will be rung, and the first muster held, at 7 o'clock, A. M. At 12 o'clock, noon, the bell will be rung, and the hour from 12 to 1 o'clock allowed for dinner, from which hour to 6 o'clock, P. M., will constitute the last half of the day.

"From the 1st day of October to the 31st day of March, the working hours will be from the rising to the setting of the sun. The bell will then be rung at one hour after sunrise, that hour being allowed for breakfast. At 12 o'clock, noon, the bell will again be rung, and one hour allowed for dinner, from which time, say 1 o'clock, till sundown, will constitute the last half of the day. No quarters of days will be allowed."

It has appeared, in evidence at the various hearings during the present discussion at the State house, that within a period ranging from two to four years of the adoption of the rule by the National Government, ten hours was established in most of the ship-building trades in this State, having been first carried into effect by the ship carpenters of Medford engaged on job work. From them it has gradually become the custom in a great portion of the labor of the cities and large towns of the

State, the labor crisis of 1853 having materially aided its final triumph, as will be seen by the following items :—

"A CARD.—The cutters of Oak Hall avail themselves of this opportunity, through the undersigned, to express their respect, regard and good-will for G. W. Simmons, Esq., for kindness, courtesy, &c.,—particularly for his generous and magnanimous free-will offer in adopting for their benefit, without waiting for or being guided by the course of others, 'The Ten-Hour System.' "JOHN MCLEOD, *Foreman.* "APRIL 14, 1853."

"At a meeting of the Mayor and Aldermen of Charlestown, April 25th, 1853, a Ten Hour ordinance was reported."—*Boston Journal,* April 28, '53.

"At a meeting of the Master Horse-shoers, an unanimous vote was passed to adopt the Ten Hour system, to go into effect next Monday." *Boston Journal, April* 30, '53.

HISTORY OF THE EIGHT HOUR MOVEMENT.

The facts connected with eight hours as a growth, precedent to its claims upon the community as a reform, are of great significance.

In a season of commercial prosperity, Boston employs some fifteen hundred or two thousand workmen, of all trades, in the repairs of her shipping.

Under the present hours of labor, but an insignificant fraction of this employ resides in the city proper ; most of it is at a distance of three miles, much of it five, and a considerable portion even further from home, impelled to such a choice of locality, by social, sanitary and pecuniary influences of an obvious character. The nature of the work is such, that it must be performed under great sacrifices of vigor, clothing, tools, and general strain upon the mental faculties. The wharves frequented by shipping, cover some six or seven miles of water-front ; work is to be reached and carried on under the difficulties of circuitous and angular routes by the ferries and bridges. Heavy boxes of tools, together with materials, are to be lugged,—the exigencies of labor not permitting to any great extent the use of teams,—much of it is performed in damp and unhealthy docks, or aloft on the masts of ships. During the heat of summer, no cooling drink can be obtained, except at luncheon time. It is notorious, that sunstroke reaps its richest harvest under the broiling temperature and exposures in which this labor is performed. The nature of much of the work is so responsible, that it can only be committed to first-class workmen of the highest physical vigor.

Nearly all the work of the caulker must be carried on in gangs, each individual being obliged to follow his predecessor, and being in his turn pressed upon by his neighbor,—failure of strength, or application, showing itself instantly by retarding the progress of all in the rear. It is well understood among workmen, that the strain upon physical and muscular energy of labor performed under such circumstances, is uniformly somewhat above the average strength of the individuals composing the group. Those momentary easements, and the variety of position, which are possible to the isolated workman, are here out of the question.

The size of vessels has so increased, as to involve large outlays of capital, both for ships and docks for their repairs. The urgency of the demand in prosperous times for shipping, compels the most rapid execution of jobs; so that expense may be lessened, and the dock be used by the next vessel upon the books. To do this, large numbers of workmen, more than can be steadily employed, must wait upon the calls of commerce.

A Board of Trade Report of about the date of 1853, says, that in Boston there is a scarcity of men, and if there is much repairing going on, not more than one-half the number of men can be obtained that might work conveniently on a vessel; so that the number of lay days is doubled, the docks charging always full price.

These statements will render intelligible the following item, which I find in the "Boston Times" of March 24th, 1853:—

"The journeymen shipwrights and caulkers of this city have increased their rate of prices to three dollars per day, commencing at eight in the morning and working till half-past five. This regulation has, we believe, been very generally agreed to, with the deduction, which is understood, of one hour at noon, and twenty minutes for luncheon; these hours are a trifle over eight per day."

Bearing in mind all the circumstances of this employ, the testimony of Mr. John Taylor, a master shipbuilder, and an opponent of the general introduction of eight hours, will be recognized as applicable. He was asked, (p. 25 of the Phonographic Reports,)—" Is business being driven out of Boston because laborers work only eight hours per day?" and answers, " There are a great many ships which go out of the place,—not particularly in consequence of the eight hours at old work, which is considered equal to ten at new, but in consequence of the extreme high prices of labor."

Rebel privateers and the war had so reduced the commerce of Boston that, for a year, at the time this testimony was taken, the caulkers had charged five dollars per day, to compensate for lost time.

To prove that the influences tending to shorten hours in Boston were not confined to a class, I quote the following item from " Hunt's Merchant's Magazine " of April, 1852 :—" A writer in a recent 'Transcript,' complains that the business hours of Boston close at two, instead of four, as in New York,—thus shortening the time for making purchases and cheapening goods. He says, very feelingly, that ' there is a loss of precious time for business purposes.' Our opinion is, if it is worth anything, that there is too much precious time lost *in* business purposes, and too little expended for higher advantages than dollars and cents.

" As people live around us, it would seem as though there was nothing but money worth living for ; and every energy of mind and body must be exercised for its attainment. Get rich, appears to be the rule that men have written on their hearts, and it is a ' waste of precious time ' to turn aside for a moment from its direction."

Those familiar with the former condition of the workmen in this business know, that it is much elevated in consequence of reduction of hours and associated effort. They are remembered as working in 1835, thirteen or fourteen hours, for $1.50 per day, confined by their hours to the city ; the younger and ruder portion formed the nucleus of Fort Hill rowdyism. There was a period when, in connection with the fire department, they kept the city in constant alarm.

From 1853 to the present season, the same class of labor is found in possession, as we have shown, of eight hours; not as a class disorderly, mostly resident in the suburbs; wages most of the time $3, rising to $4, and for a short time, and, as we have seen under peculiar circumstances, to $5 per day.

The President of the Caulker's Association has recently stated, under circumstances precluding bias, that one-third of them were men of property.

The history of the eight-hour movement in Boston will not be complete without a notice of the labor crisis of the summer of 1866 :—

"A large and enthusiastic meeting of the workingmen of Boston and vicinity, assembled in the old Cradle of Liberty on Monday evening, July 2d, to hear a true statement of the case of the caulker's lock-out, to tender aid, and to take such counsel and action as the exigency might seem to require of the friends of labor.

"The president of the evening, Col. C. G. Rowell of East Boston, on taking the chair briefly expressed thanks for the honor conferred, and then introduced Mr. Charles E. Turner, President of the Boston Caulker's Association. Mr. Turner, in his remarks, wanted it distinctly understood that this was no strike of the caulkers, but a lock-out of the shipowners and builders. The shipwrights and caulkers of New York on the 2d of April last, struck for eight hours a day. The ship Archer was sent from New York to Boston to be repaired,—because the owners would not let the work be done in New York on the eight-hour system, and were determined to defeat the strike. We were pledged to assist our fellow-craftsmen. We had worked for fifteen years on the eight-hour system, and wanted not only to continue that system, but to help others to do it. The Archer had a charter in New York, and when asked to repair her, we answered that we would work on her if the owners would allow New York caulkers to come and assist, at eight hours a day. This was refused, and we could not, therefore, in justice to ourselves, or our fellow-craftsmen, consent to work on her. We were therefore locked out, by conditions which we could not accept— four dollars a day for nine hours work."

The state of labor in New York at this time will be understood by the following preamble, adopted in connection with resolutions at a meeting of shipbuilders, master shipwrights, and joiners, of New York and vicinity :—

"*Whereas*, The ship-carpenters, joiners and caulkers, of New York and vicinity, have demanded that eight hours, instead of ten, shall constitute a day's labor, and have refused to work until their demands shall be acceded to; and have, by means of their organization, and threats of personal violence, driven away many who wished to continue under the old regulations,—thereby depriving by force a large number of families of their livelihood, and inflicting upon us—their employers—serious inconvenience, besides damaging the commercial community by endeavoring so to raise the price of labor, that it would be impossible for New York to compete with other seaports in the building and repairing of vessels; and, whereas, we consider ten hours as no more than a fair day's work, at the present high prices paid therefor; and, that their demand is unwise and unjust, and, at the same time, ruinous to us and the merchants, without benefiting themselves; and, whereas, we, &c."

The view which the Boston shipowners took is expressed in the following resolution, one of a series adopted at the rooms of the Boston Board of Trade, June 8th, 1866 :—

"*Resolved*, That a refusal to work under such circumstances, when no dictation has been attempted as to the number of hours which shall constitute a day's work, and no dispute as to the price which shall be paid per day for labor, is, in the opinion of this meeting, a proceeding which cannot, and ought not to be sustained, and one which no circumstances can justify or approve."

The present hours of this employ are explained by an extract from " Rules and Regulations for the future government of Merchants, Shipwrights, and Caulkers : "

" Whereas, contrary to the wishes of the merchants and master shipwrights of Boston, they have been compelled, by the refusal of the Boston caulkers to work on the ship Archer, or to allow others to work, either on said ship Archer or other vessels, for our own protection, we do hereby solemnly agree to the following, namely :

" 2. That we will employ no dock, railway, or master mechanic, that will not make hours and price the same as expressed in these articles.

" 3. Work to commence at 8, A. M.; one hour at dinner; and to work until 6, P. M., or sunset, if before 6, P. M."

Lack of time prevents me from tracing the legislative history of labor, beyond an allusion to the able reports on the subject of Factory labor of the Hon. James M. Stone and William S. Robinson, Esq., years 1850 and 1852, (House Documents 153 and 185.)

CAUSES AND CONNECTIONS OF THE EIGHT-HOUR MOVEMENT.

The most influential motives of a practical character in the eight-hour movement are to be found in the altered conditions of labor, incidental to the monotony of subdivision, and the intensity of application enforced by the state of society. The rapidity of completion of many undertakings, causing the workman frequent changes of location, and expenditure of time and strength in travel, and that development of character which makes him dislike the cramped accommodations of the great cities, resulting, in its connection with travelling facilities, in residence at a distance from labor; the prevalence, among thoughtful workingmen, of more definite views respecting manual labor, whether its characteristics should be those of skill and faithfulness, or unreasoning endurance; a clearer recognition of the effect of continuous physical effort on the action of the mind and its capacity, and also on the condition of the workman, as being in an exhausted state during his brief space of leisure; a comparison of the more favored conditions of mercantile and professional life, as affording educational influences during the day, and leaving the body comparatively free from fatigue, to engage with zest and energy in the social privileges or duties of the evening; a conviction that the returns for labor under the present system are not adequate to the reasonable and necessary demands of American citizenship; —these motives, with others, resulting in great unanimity of opinion, that radical reductions of hours are necessary to place labor in its just relations to the other interests of society. In connection with these points, I propose an inquiry into the nature and immediate effects of physical labor.

Adopting, as suitable to the present purpose, the definition of Mr. Beecher, that "Work is the application of human physical force to matter," I clear myself at once from much of the declamation upon the subject, and reach the roots of the matter, by reference to the divine statement of its character after the loss of primal innocence. In consequence of sin, the ground was cursed, and Adam was doomed to eat bread in the sweat of his face. We are not required to take this sentence as absolute or irrevocable. A liberal construction warrants the conclusion that it is in the estimation and circumstances of labor, rather than in its essential character, that it has been regarded or has proved a curse or burden. To the extent that the first estate of man is restored by advancing righteousness, labor takes, by its ameliorations, rewards and considerations, the position designed for it by the Creator,—an honorable one, as having vital relations with all human excellence and progress. We cannot suppose the two volumes, in which God reveals himself, to disagree.

The results of a reasonable amount of labor upon the system are too manifestly beneficial to doubt the character of nature's utterance; and for the combined effect on mind and body, I have never found a sentence more practical and comprehensive than the one alluded to in the sketch of Channing's views on questions of labor: —"*Manual labor is a school in which men are placed to get energy of purpose and character.*" Taken in connection with his further expression of opinion, "Manual labor is a great good; but, in so saying, I must be understood to speak of labor in its just proportions; in excess, it does great harm," we have an apology, if one is needed, for the movement to reduce the hours of labor.

If we consider that it is the passions which in the main give "energy of purpose," we shall see that however beneficial labor may be in its productive results, and as compared with the nerveless inefficiency and moral hazard of idleness, it bears along with it deprivations and exposures to evil of a momentous character.

Stated in another form, the pith of Channing's axiom seems to be that the preponderance which is given to the development of the body by healthful labor, in connection with the training of the volition and will to accomplish practical results in spite of obstacles, acts directly, by the intimacy of the union between the base of the brain and the bodily functions, to stimulate the passions.

But if it is true that labor gives its force to passion, it is also certain that fatigue waits closely on her steps to hold in constraint the impulses of our lower nature. Few features of humble life are more noticeable than the fact, that it is the excess of leisure, of the sailor on shore, or the laborer out of work, that unlooses the appetites, and sends them on their course of indulgence. In this connection, the loss on the part of labor seems to be, that the force of daily culture is diverted from all the gentler, pleasing, imaginative sentiments, and distinctively intellectual and spiritual faculties and capacities. I mean, of course, so far as labor is concerned, not having the slightest motive to deny the preponderating influence on all the higher industrial element, of the means for good from other sources.

The failure to appreciate this difference between mental, and manual labor, constitutes one of the chief obstacles to an amicable settlement of the question in dispute. "I often work more than ten hours," says the employer, without the slightest idea, that there is a radical, as well as a circumstantial difference between the two descriptions of activity, going back for its causes to the reason I have named. The ingenious and well-disposed youth in our public schools, whose tendencies of mind lead him almost irresistibly to the exercise of a life of constructive skill, little realizes the marked injustice of our prevailing ideas, nor is it usually until maturity that he learns that it would have been better for him to follow the current in the determination to avoid productive labor.

Admission to the confidence of respectable workingmen, reveals incidents quite explicit on this point. "Why do you leave the counting room?" said an influential Sabbath school teacher, a few years since, to a young man, a member of his class. "I leave for reasons connected with my health, and the incongeniality of mercantile life!" "You cannot support a family as a mechanic, and under the burdens of labor your abilities will be lost to society."

Such are the influences which are making our schools and other social facilities, by a large share of their power, weights upon our industrial system, instead of helps to it. Of what avail is it that the agents of our great corporations, put in their testimony in favor of educated labor, under a state of things which induces on the score of self-respect and social estimation, a large part of that labor, into unproductive channels, or disperses it to the four quarters of the globe in emigration.

I shall allude elsewhere to the effects of the concentration of capital, in shutting out the most intelligent portion of labor from independent positions. In the progress of society this class is called upon to furnish candidates for public duties, of a nature not calling for the suspension of their daily labor. Do they meet on terms of equality, in respect to physical condition, their fellow-citizens of mercantile and professional engagements? I do not claim that business men are not overworked; but it is true that, as a rule, their time in the cities is considerably shorter than workmen. A fact develops itself here of great moment, in its tendencies to perpetuate class distinctions. Our indiscriminate estimate of the situation of labor, in view of these responsibilities is seen, when we consider the difference in bodily vigor of the two interests of society after the day's employment. The mind, in both cases, may be weary, but mind in its nature admits of recuperation by change of theme; but for the exhausted workman, there is no relief short of yielding to nature's claim for repose.

Society is thus deprived of the services of a large class of her most energetic, and, in many cases, most intelligent citizens, as in these circumstances none but those of unusual bodily vigor can accept these places, or fulfil their duties.

From the elemental truth thus laid down by commanding authority, confirmed by the testimony which has been developed, and which is urged with emphasis by the toiling masses in the present agitation, I infer that manual labor beyond a minimum of daily duration, which is not likely to be reached at present, is sacrificial in its character, injurious in some of its results to the individual, and as such in all its higher relations, has claims upon society for consideration in the inauguration of rules and customs.

Reviewing the developments of popular feeling during the last fifteen years, we find that the present interest is partly the result of reactionary tendencies from the exclusive claims upon the public mind, of the contest between the North and South, and partly the result of a higher standard of manliness developed by the war. Patriotism and policy alike, combined to suppress, or at least postpone, the effort of the operative population of the State, during the first half of the decade from

1850 to 1860 to obtain the ten hour-day of labor. In the interim, the country has been moved by a deep emotive experience, in connection with events of the greatest magnitude. More than two million of men, mostly producers, have been relieved from the ordinary conditions of labor, under circumstances and with results which have told influentially on the present movement. It is a fact worth noting, that where large numbers are employed, influences are developed tending to shorten time. These forces seem to operate above the usual plane of commercial motives, and the more elevated and comprehensive the authority is, the more marked the result. The city of Lawrence is one of the last expressions of the mind of the capitalists of the Athens of America; and, at the present writing, her time is the shortest of the manufacturing cities of the State, 10¾ hours, the quarter hour being a recent concession of a most grateful character to the claims of the stomach at the noon repast. In contrast with this, the individual owners and small corporations of the western portion of the State, have but just reduced their time from twelve to eleven hours. One reason of this I take to be, that the injurious effects of long hours are more evident in large concerns, and appeal more directly to an elevated sense of utility for an immediate remedy.

In the army, professional skill, unembarrassed by pecuniary bligations, has been very largely in control in all the minutiæ of sanitary regulations. Thousands of citizen soldiers, of quick perception and enlarged intelligence, have observed with deep interest the difference for the better in the army regulations. The two hours of morning, and three hours of afternoon drill, in the usual routine, are relieved by frequent intervals of rest; and in all circumstances, except those imminent in their nature, from five to eight hours of fatigue work are the customs established by experience in the handling of large bodies of troops. The alternations of time in guard duty, and exemption on the day succeeding, are further developments in the same direction.

Workmen and women are held under the present customs and ideas to at least five hours each half day of continuous work, often in the most tedious, minute and monotonous employ. It is assumed, in many instances, that they have no lower limbs to ache with swollen or ruptured veins, no delicacy of nerve, or versatility of mind, to revolt from such severity of application, with a protest which derives force and volume from the multiplied educational influences of the day. Our fathers established the rule, that it should be considered indecorous to sit during labor hours when it was possible to stand ; and so the plainest dictates of physiology must be disregarded in industrial life. The manuals of advice placed in the hands of our soldiers, exhorted them to relieve their feet as often as they could, and their first day's drill found the humane idea enforced by the order " rest," than which none was more emphatic or needful.

The traditions of centuries have thus been jostled from their hold on a large number of our people, by the rude but effective hand of war. Their overthrow has been synonymous with the profound experiences of military exposure. Multitudes have sharply tested social anomalies, amid the most impressive scenes, and give at least a portion of their conclusions in adherence to this reform.

The character of the present discussion will be injuriously misapprehended, if its leading motives are taken to be care for mere physical well-being. With exalted prescience of the true issues in the dispute, Dr. Channing, speaking of the lower element of labor, has said,—" It is not the physical suffering of the poor, but their relation to the rest of society, the want of means of inward life, the lowering influences of their position, to which their chief misery is to be traced." An able advocate of reform, Mr. Ira Steward, in a letter to the present Commission has well said,—" The reasons which were given in the twelve and fourteen hour system for reducing to ten, are not reasons which have much weight for the proposed eight-hour reduction. There is as much difference between the class of arguments for the two systems, ten and eight hours, as between the reasoning which is especially adapted to the movement for giving the slave his freedom, and the later one, of giving the freeman a ballot."

Ten hours has been proved in its adoption by the masses of needy and not specially intellectual laborers, to be in the interests of the body. Dr. Jarvis admits that he has simply muscular effort in view, when he says that men can work ten hours a day without impairing health. The present movement seems, by its sequence and connections with the double nature of man, likely to reveal itself to be the first step of a change in the condition of the masses of a generic character.

The arbitrary power of a despot could not have consummated the growth of that agreeable feature of our civilization, —our suburban towns and cities. Railroads alone would never have accomplished it. The vitality of the force which, in twenty-five years, has brought it quietly about, may all be packed in the line, "Ten hours in Boston, sent her shopkeepers, artisans, &c., to the suburbs." They have crowded the environs, and the demand is for more time and more room, to meet the varied wants of this distinctive, national development.

Any one who will visit the second tier of the localities encircling the city, such as North Chelsea, Malden, Medford, &c., will find extensive tracts of land, which has passed out of cultivation, and has been surveyed for the residence of those classes who do business in the city, but has been lying on the market, without purchasers, for an indefinite period. The general community seem to have very vague ideas as to the capacity of the body to endure fatigue. In this case, these views have operated disastrously, as these lands are not likely to be occupied, with the present hours of labor.

The American mind is penetrating and forceful in its character; it rejects the idea that the day of labor, which has come to us without intelligent consideration, from the darkness and oppression of the past, shall continue to throw its pall over the noble faculties of manhood. The scanty schooling received in the country, barely meets the ordinary exigencies of existence among the hosts who fight the battle of life in the intensity of thought, feeling and effort in our cities. We have mistaken the rudiments of knowledge for knowledge itself. There is an instinctive and wide-spread feeling among these classes, that broad institutions and new customs must be initiated to meet the demands of the times. The mind of the scholar is expanded and strengthened by mathematical and classical study. The commercial interests receive an education, defective it is true, in the exercise of their pursuits. Continuous application through the day to study or inquiry is out of the question for the masses. But, under the proposed reduction of hours, mental culture would not be cramped and straitened by confinement to the evenings of two or three winter months. "Knowledge would open her ample page," unchecked by any interruption, except that of midsummer.

Take the science of geology, specially in its relation to time, as it has been recorded upon the rocks, as legibly as a dial; how impressive in its liberalizing influence on the mind. Place a class of intelligent workingmen in any place of moderate size, under the instruction of a person tolerably well versed in its principles, for the evenings of nine months and as long as they should continue to reside in that place its affairs would be sensibly relieved of a petty narrowness, almost inseparable from present circumstances. Gross ignorance pervades the community, in reference to the truths of physiology. The relations of such themes as ventilation, bathing, &c., to health and prosperity, lie on the extreme of the horizon of the industrial classes.

In another direction, a science formerly deemed the most abstruse, yet one of daily and of universal need, is republicanized in the truths of phrenology. The people occasionally hear of these matters in lectures, but they need them as practical knowledge, to develop capacities now dormant.

> "For as our vineyards, fallows, meads and hedges,
> Defective in their natures, grow to wildness;
> Even so our houses, and ourselves and children,
> Have lost, or do not learn, for want of time,
> The sciences that should become our country."

The popular opposition to science has been removed; the next step is to graft it upon the daily life of the masses. A letter in the "National Trades Review," an organ of labor published in Philadelphia, shows its connection with human life and comfort:—

"SIR:—Now I see that there is a person trying to get air into the coal mines, and in vain do I look for some reply being made to his call upon miners to come forth and tell, or give their opinions, on this important matter. My husband has been troubled with asthma for several years, and as he is a miner, and is obliged to come out and come home on every occasion when the mines are full of powder smoke, it does seem strange to me that so many miners, all over the country, and no one of them to answer the call of this person, to try to make it better for the poor men who suffer so much for want of air all the year round in some of the coal mines. Excuse me, sir, for troubling you, but I do think that there are both mine employers and men, workers in the mines, that ought to come forward and give their opinion, and try to help in this case. My husband cannot write, or he would have done so, since you are so kind as to publish working-people's letters from all over the country; and as you say, in July 8th paper, that it is in consequence of people not writing that you are publishing novelettes, &c.

Excuse me, sir, for troubling you, for I feel it is scarcely a woman's duty to speak or write on this matter, where there must be so many men interested in so important a matter as to get pure air to breathe in their dangerous calling. I am, yours truly,

SALLY M———."

In the same direction, Horace Mann, writing in 1842, says:—

"For the last ten years, such have been the disastrous fluctuations of our National and State policy, on the single subject of the currency, that all the prodigality of nature, pouring her hundreds of millions of products annually into our hands, has not been able to save thousands of our people from poverty; and, in many cases, economy, industry and virtue could not rescue their possessor from want. And, why? I answer, because this question has been decided, again and again, by voters to whom the simplest question in political economy or national finance is as unintelligible as a book of Hebrew or Greek."

The same great mind in his Lectures on Education, (p. 123,) strikingly delineates the needs of our times:—

"Now it is undeniable that, with the possession of certain higher faculties,—common to all mankind,—whose proper cultivation will bear us upward to hitherto undiscovered regions of prosperity and glory, we possess, also, certain lower faculties or propensities, equally common whose improper indulgence leads inevitably, to tribulation, and anguish, and ruin. The propensities to which I refer, seem indispensable to our temporal existence, and if restricted within proper limits, they are promotive of our enjoyment; but beyond those limits, they work dishonor and infatuation, madness and despair. As servants, they are indispensable; as masters, they torture as well as tyrannize. Now despotic and arbitrary governments have dwarfed and crippled the powers of doing evil as much as the powers of doing good; but a republican government, from the very fact of its freedom, unreins their speed, and lets loose their strength. It is justly alleged against despotisms, that they fetter, mutilate, almost extinguish the noblest powers of the human soul; but there is a *per contra* to this, for which we have not given them credit: they circumscribe the ability to do the greatest evil, as well as to do the greatest good.

"My proposition, therefore, is simply this: If republican institutions do wake up unexampled energies in the whole mass of a people, and give them implements of unexampled power wherewith to work out their will; then these same institutions ought also to confer upon that people unexampled wisdom and rectitude. If these institutions give greater scope and impulse to the lower order of faculties belonging to the human mind, then they must also give more authoritative control, and more skilful guidance to the higher ones. If they multiply temptations, they must fortify against them. If they quicken the activity and enlarge the sphere of the appetites and passions, they must at least in an equal ratio establish the authority and extend the jurisdiction of reason and conscience. In a word, we must not add to the impulsive, without also adding to the regulating forces.

"If we maintain institutions which bring us within the action of new and unheard of powers, without taking any corresponding measures for the government of these powers, we shall perish by the very instruments prepared for our happiness."

Social Elevation.

The change from a standard of labor whose highest merit seems to be that it is deemed the maximum of production, to one acknowledged to be educational in its character, will, it is fair to presume, introduce compensations hitherto unthought of.

Testimony deemed worthy the consideration of statesmen was brought forward during the discussion of the factory bill in England, proving that many of the operatives lessened the number of their meals from twenty-six to twenty-one per week, immediately after the reduction to ten hours; thus demonstrating the instant operation of influences almost purely physical, in the direction of a more economical style of living.

Much of the sharp criticism of the working classes in respect to excessive eating, seems to have been inconsiderate. We infer this from recollection of the tone of society before any change in hours was effected. Nothing was more common than to hear from influential sources, comments on this proclivity of workmen. These remarks were not usually calculated to convince the judgment, or produce good feeling between the different interests of society. It seems now to be admitted, tacitly at least, that the public judgment was defective, and that the distillery and the shambles had no more effective allies than they found in days of twelve to fourteen hours duration.

Much more intelligent, as well as charitable, is the verdict which Mrs. Kirkland passes upon the Western farmers, when she says in speaking of their gross feeding at their harvest time, that any other course than fourteen hours of labor, with such eating, would be suicidal.

Those workmen who are in the habit of subjecting their daily routine to the test of reason and morals, acknowledge with regret the extreme difficulty of controlling the desire for food. The large populations of our suburbs, average fourteen hours of continuous activity, with the exception of a brief interval at noon. The exhausted condition of all who are in laborious callings, and to a very considerable extent of the rest, concentrates intense desire upon the gratification of the appetite at the evening meal. Torpor and sleepiness soon follow, by the operation of laws inevitably connected with such prolonged and unseasonable exercise of the physical functions of labor and nutrition. The two hours that society allows to the mass of its members for the fulfilment of the fundamental duties of the church, the state, and the family, are neutralized, if not reversed in their direction, by the burdens of excessive appetite and extreme fatigue.

Such conditions of daily life cannot be without their injurious influence on public affairs. And accordingly we find intervals, during which it is impossible to rouse the people to a calm sense of responsibility, succeeded by periodic convulsions of such character as to repel the moderate and thoughtful from participation in politics.

The manifestations of religion, sympathize from time to time with the passionate intensity or the sluggish indifference thus ingrained by daily habits into the character and tendencies of the community.

A noble literature, which ought to be in daily contact with the minds and hearts of the people, is neglected, or substituted by the stimulating reading necessitated by mental habits in harmony with such unintellectual training.

One of the noticeable developments of modern times is seen in the constant movement upwards into what is usually termed genteel society, of individuals so numerous as to constitute classes. Hitherto these additions to the polite or influential element of society have been mainly from the class of tradesmen or mechanics in artistic callings.

The aggregation of labor in the cities is tending to the growth of higher conditions of life in trades which twenty-five years ago were positively averse to all the minutiæ of observance and the denials of impulse which are required in good society. The possession of two hours of leisure, has brought the careless and impulsive workman in contact with his superiors in culture, in in the daily ride in the car, and in social gatherings of manifold descriptions; privileges which formerly were impossible.

Thirty years ago, the daily use of the tooth-brush by a workman was without precedent. It is remembered that a laboring community but a short distance from Boston were moved to alternate ridicule or indignation at this innovation on the part of one of their members. Abundant evidence is accessible proving the advance in the ideas of cleanliness and refinement implied in this extension of the popular toilet. The sale of the tooth-brush by our fancy-goods dealers is not confined to any class, and army sutlers say that its use was frequent in regiments recruited from the least cultured of our people.

In harmony with these statements, is the desire felt by a large and increasing number of workingmen to modify existing customs of dress. Why is it that the surgeon, or student in the dissecting-room, or the active partner or salesman in the wholesale druggist's or flour store, preserve their social standing in spite of the untoward nature of their callings? To a great extent, we hold, because their time is not so inflexibly the property of others, as to shut them up to the necessity of rushing into the street in such a garb as to lose their self-respect. Undoubtedly other influences mingle here; but it is unquestionably true that the advance in social proprieties, is forcing upon workingmen a sense of their straitened situation in this respect not formerly felt. Everywhere in our shops is seen the stringent regulation forbidding the cessation of labor before " time is up."

From a quarter to half an hour is needed for a thorough cleansing and change of clothing in many of the offensive and uncleanly trades. The situation of a large portion of our labor is such that a social cordon is drawn around it from this cause alone. If the community are willing to allow class distinctions to disappear, they must ultimately consent to an amelioration of time. Such is the tendency of our nature to be influenced by appearances, that much greater weight must be given to an improvement of this character in elevating labor than to other changes intrinsically more important.

As we have already partially shown, foremost among the means of class elevation is the reduction of the expenses of the table. While a rude community boasts of profusion in this respect, a refined one, or one tending in that direction, recognizes that here is cost and labor which must be brought within the narrowest limits. The example of the adult workers of the family, impelled to free indulgence of the appetite by the present hours, influences the rest as to render it practically impossible for them to differ; so that habits and expenses are engrafted on the whole household. Members of trades the most influential in former movements have learned that their ability to gratify elevated tastes is sensibly aided by reductions of hours, both by moderation of appetite, time for attention to personal and home affairs, and facilities for purchases of food and clothing.

These revelations of the every-day life of the industrial classes have, if we mistake not, extended and significant connections with other interest of society; their inherent character is such as to be prophetic of larger room for the press, the lecture, music, and the graces which adorn cultivated society, and these anticipations seem still further favored by the following views, which I abridge from an article in the United States Agricultural Report for 1863, page 248:—

" Whatever constantly aids the progress of civilization, however feeble its force, is of vital importance to a community. But whenever anything is found that exerts a controlling power, it ought to be carefully investigated, and thoroughly examined in all its bearings.

" The supply of food occupies the larger portion of the energies of the human race; and it must be provided for in all communities to secure their prosperity, happiness and advancement. If the constitution of a community is such that all its energies are absorbed in the production of food and clothing, all its sources of improvement will remain closed, and the community will be at a standstill. No time is left to cultivate the mind, and from exhaustive physical labor, it readily relapses into a state of barbarism.

" On the other hand, when a community is so constituted that all its energies are not required to feed and clothe its citizens, the mind is cultivated, sources of prosperity multiply, and the nation gradually rises to the highest rank in the civilized world.

" In the United States, our fertile and extensive agricultural lands, while covered with a comparatively sparse population, have yielded fabulous crops from a virgin soil. Large profits being thus easily obtained, it has not been deemed necessary to husband resources, and the soil has been allowed to become exhausted, thus creating large tracts of so-called worn-out lands in a great number of States. In a similar manner many aids to civilization may be carelessly neglected, and although advancement may not be at the time perceptibly checked, it will soon become apparent. Hence the agriculturist should avail himself of every means of information within his reach, that he may carefully gather up all the varied resources of his country, and reduce the time and strength necessary for the production of food and clothing within the smallest limits, thereby giving greater scope to the developement and enjoyment of his and his country's intellectual and moral forces.

" In this view, the importance which is attached to the agricultural interests of a country is more clearly comprehended. The greater the improvements made in implements of agriculture, the more completely the crops are adapted to the soil and climate, the more the facilities of communication are increased, and the more accurately the agricultural statistics of a nation are obtained, the more will the nation advance with all its other interests.

" To aid in this general developement, by discovering some of the statistics gathered by the census bureau, is the object of the present article."

The writer proceeds to show by voluminous tables, that every one hundred people require eighty neat cattle yearly for laboring purposes and for food; that in 1860 Massachusetts had but one-quarter of the requisite number, and that her production of cattle had been constantly decreasing for twenty years, while the point of greatest productiveness had been steadily moving westward at the rate of 500 miles in ten years.

Speaking of the statistics of 1860, he says, "We are led to infer a general reduction in the entire country east of the Mississippi River, with an occasional exception, while our great herds still gather around the pioneers, as, pushing westward, they lay the foundations of civilized life in the dominions of the savage."

Instruction in Labor.

Man differs from all other creatures, in his relation to nature.

"His predominant, and governing principle, is intelligence. The insect, as soon as it arrives at the perfect state, is capable of all of which it is ever capable; it goes through no education, it makes no improvement, it does not learn by experience, it is taught nothing by its parents, it teaches nothing to its offspring, — nothing is transmitted from generation to generation. The race is where it was thousands of years ago. On the contrary, at birth, man knows nothing, he can do nothing. He has only powers and tendencies which are latent. Beginning by actions which are instinctive, and an education which is also instinctive, his intelligence becomes gradually developed; it is informed by education, observation, and experience; and at length assumes the principal control over his life. He learns from his parents. He teaches his children, and the accumulated treasure of one generation is transmitted to the next."

A system of labor, which neglects, or undervalues these primary conditions of being, must be defective. That we have at the present time, anything deserving the name of a system, or even custom of training in productive labor, would hardly be claimed by any one.

The following extracts, from a recent petition to the legislature, will show the present condition of the arts in this respect, with some of the moral connections:—

"The undersigned, members of the producing classes, represent to your Honorable Body, the inconveniences we suffer, in common, from a defective Apprentice system.

" Lads are placed at trades, without indenture, which leaves it optional with them to remain and obtain a perfect knowledge of the business; and masters are equally free to send them out upon the world, as perfect or imperfect workmen.

" By the simple contract system, boys leave their places, and flee from one shop to another without restraint, assuming mature positions in early youth, to the great danger of their morality and usefulness as men, and too frequently deficient in a knowledge of the trade they essay to learn.

"Without the restraint of law, and holding themselves amenable to neither parent or master, the mechanical arts suffer, propriety is too often shocked, and society is demoralized. It is deteriorating from the excellency of mechanical arts, and lowering the American standard of perfection; which secures to Europe, an advantage that must disparage the prospect of American mechanics.

" We claim, that to the present loose apprenticeship system, can be traced many accidents on our railroads, steamboats, bridges, and in mining regions, as well as imperfections in the manufacturing, and agricultural interests."

The substantial truth of these positions, as well as others, which I have omitted, was with great clearness, shown before the joint committee of 1865, on the hours of labor, and the apprenticeship system, and formed the base of views embodied in House Doc., No. 256, of that year.

We hear much of the neglect of physical training. Its benefits are sought for in active games in the gymnasium, rowing, &c. Really the remedy is to be found in such comprehensive measures in the regulation of labor, as will retain a larger portion of our youth in production, under healthful circumstances, and relieve the less onerous callings from the existing pressure of those who crowd them, merely to escape the burdens, and odium of labor in its present condition.

Relying upon the axiom " that labor is the divine training to energize the character," it is but a step to the inference, that by its means, the body should receive that thorough development, necessary to place it in harmony with the mind. Viewed in this light, the physical degeneracy, so characteristic of the cities, appears simply as a divine rebuke, for the unsound conditions of labor, which sends the sons of our respectable artisans, and farmers, *en masse*, into mercantile life.

From " Moore's Rural New-Yorker " of recent date, I take an article on " Physical Education " :—

"The general neglect of physical training, is among the strangest of strange things. *The utter absence of any plan, provision, or arrangement, for teaching boys or girls how to work, when work is at the bottom of all material interests, is the real wonder of the world.* Painful as the truth is, there is no doubt but a very large per cent. of all human physical efforts, are thrown away, by not knowing 'how to do it.' This amounts to a loss of untold millions, in productive returns, and a waste of time, more precious than all the gold of Australia. Human strength, which ought to be developed, and preserved, with assiduous care, and applied with the soundest discretion to the great objects and necessities of human life, is thus, to a large extent, utterly wasted.

"We can judge in some measure of the magnitude of this loss, by observing the difference between skilled and unskilled labor,—by watching a green-horn chopper, who never hits twice in the same place, and whose blow falls dead from not having the right direction, the peculiar slant and sleight, that dexterous workmen know so well how to give. It is notorious that you may take two men of equal power, one carefully educated, and practised in the use of the axe, and the other not,—and the former will cut three logs off while the latter is cutting one. I have often seen it tried.

"There is one point of great weight in this connection, generally overlooked. The beginner, when left to himself, *confirms by practice the objectionable style which he first adopts.* He drills himself in; he hardens himself, and he pertinaceously perseveres, till he makes tolerable progress at his work; but he has only modified his errors, and he will go through life, expending a third more strength, and accomplishing a third less labor, than the man who is introduced to right methods at the start. The agony endured by men and boys, who have the size and strength, and the ambition to 'keep up,' but who work to a disadvantage, is really pitiful. They conceal their weariness, and pains, strike hard and often, watching the tardy sun, which seems to stand still, in mockery of their woe. Call it ambition, or pride, or chivalry, or folly, or what you will; multitudes of our most athletic and spirited young men—these are the very ones—break down: the victims of disease, and pain, and premature death, in consequence of the insane practice of beginning the work of life, before they have learned how to work."

In another article from the same source, the relations of productive labor to the individual and society, are argued in a manner forcibly illustrating the principles I have made as fundamental:—

"Something like half of our active hours should be spent in physical effort; the body demands it imperatively; omit it, and physical and intellectual degeneracy follow; the bones will lack firmness and strength,—the muscles will be deficient in size and power,—the digestive organs, the lungs, the brain, the skin, the blood, the nerves, will all be feeble and faulty in their action, and gradually succumb to disease and premature death.

"A really strong man, healthy and developed in body and mind, must sleep eight hours every day; rest and recreate four hours; give six hours to mental and moral labor and discipline, and six hours to vigorous bodily activity. Any material change in this programme, dwarfs body or mind, or both.

"I have brought this matter up at this time for the purpose of saying, that labor is an indispensable element in human affairs, and therefore (ought to be) eminently reputable.

"All who would not live a lingering death, must spend a large portion of their time in some kind of active exercise. Therefore it is immensely important that this enlarged and indispensable bodily activity should be turned into productive channels.

"Vagrant wanderers for health, rich or poor, quartering themselves upon hard-working people, are criminals before the higher law. Whoever walks five miles for exercise, when he could gain just as much by hoeing five rows of corn, steals from nature's treasury, and God will put him on his trial yet. Sports may do for children, but a full grown man or woman, whose mind and heart are not diseased, will demand and find activities all the more healthful and healing, from the consciousness of their adding to the store of good things for man. With immense harvests to be gathered, and as things now stand, crushing labors to be performed, I address these considerations to all 'sedentary' people, and all outside the pale of productive industry.

"It is worthy of prompt and profound consideration, whether professional men, mechanics, bankers, artists, idlers, should not bestir themselves with determined energy to find homes with lands for cultivation attached. If they are not found in the cities, it merely proves that the cities are the wrong places to live in. Farming is 'drudgery,' and is denied comforts and embellishments,—because farmers are saddled with labors that others ought to divide with them. God is not to be cheated; he works with a purpose, and so must we."

I infer then from my premises, thus supported by facts and arguments, that there is a marked omission in our social arrangements. Closely examined in its connections and results, it will be seen to be serious, if not alarming. Thousands of youths among us, by circumstance for which they cannot be said to be to blame, are divorced, to a great extent, from the ties and restraints of home, by transfer from the country to a city life, and other thousands by the place of their birth, which has shaken their relation to conservative forms of religious belief, are adrift in all their moral connections. The terms of complacency with which Mr. Warden Haynes, in his report for 1866, alludes to those discharged from the State prison, after learning trades, speaks volumes in favor of a reform in this respect, in its effects on the morals of a community :—

"One great advantage possessed by the prison is the facility of teaching the prisoners, (eighty per cent. of whom have no trades when received,) some useful trade, so that when they learn they may obtain employment at good wages,—which many of them do, and become honest, industrious and thriving citizens."

This illustration loses none of its force, when we consider that a large part of our crime is committed by a class so depressed that they cannot by social means obviate the evils to which they are exposed by this industrial deficiency.

The first generation of foreign parentage must necessarily be more exposed to temptation, by being forced to meet the hard conditions of their lot without the advice and aid of intelligent connections, and deprived of the advantages which a system of labor under instruction would give them. Take the case of a young man employed in a boiler shop, in iron ship-building, in the machine shop, or foundry, in any of the elementary processes of manipulation of iron; how discouraging his situation; swinging a heavy hammer, without intermission or change, ten hours each day, year in and year out, with such noise as to forbid conversation; held by scanty wages to the steadiest employ, or suffering pecuniarily from occasional relaxation; he has an instinctive sense that some share of the lighter and more varied work which he sees going on around him ought to be his, but through defects which we have seen to be common to the race, he cannot perform it. No way is provided for his training; if he wishes to go up he must accept less pay. Of the means at the disposal of this class of youths to do this, some judgment may be formed, when I say that it was found necessary to except nearly one-half of the men in government employ in the navy yard, a few years since, when a voluntary collection was being made in aid of the National Home for Seamen. Or in other words, all whose wages were not over two dollars per day.

Nor are the moral evils of this deficiency confined to the humbler classes of labor. The report already alluded to, states that even in the most favorable circumstances, that of hand work in trades not admitting of minute subdivision, the proportion of skilled workmen was but one-third of any number usually found together. And in the large majority of cases it was much less. It cannot be said that these trades do not require and admit wise regulations.

Strong, if not decisive collateral evidence in the direction of these views, is afforded by the tendencies of influential organizations, to recognize, and in a limited way, remedy this great deficiency.

The " New York Evening Post," in an article on the practices of marine insurance companies, speaks of the want of some system of examination for those who are to be made masters of vessels :—

"In 1860, an organized attempt was made by influential ship-owners, merchants, and underwriters, which resulted in the establishment of the American Ship-masters' Association, an institution chartered by the legislature of New York, for the purpose of examining, and certifying to the qualification of masters and officers of vessels. The plan met with very general favor, and the association is now permanently established.

"It has upon its published register about four thousand names, and on the list are to be found very many of those who have taken the highest rank as shipmasters. It proved of important service to the government during the war ; and its members were well represented in the ranks of our volunteer navy. Applicants for a certificate of the Shipmasters' Association, are examined by competent persons, in seamanship and navigation, and the reports submitted to a committee of experienced shipmasters. Each commission issued, bears a number, which is not changed ; and this is used as a signal, somewhat upon the system adopted ted in the commercial code ; or simply by exhibiting a blue flag with a red border, on which the number of the master's commission appears. A book, or register, is printed, which gives every number the name corresponding to it, and the name of the vessel to which the holder of each commission is attached. Thus, at sea, as far as the flag can be seen, and the number made out, an intelligible signal is readily made. What we now need, beside the Shipmasters' Association, or in connection with it, is some well-planned system of apprenticeship for ship's boys. It is to the interest of masters, and owners, that boys should be apprenticed to the ship, or to her commander, rather than to be loosely changed from ship to ship with the sailors. But in order to keep apprentices faithful, they must be made to feel that their interests are cared for by the owner whom they serve. The law should secure to them during their apprenticeship, thorough education in seamanship and navigation, and custom should prescribe, as his best interests certainly do, that from his apprentices, the ship-owner should select the officers to manage and command his vessels."

A writer in the "New York Times" refers to the large number of lives, annually sacrificed in our merchant service, by falling from aloft, when engaged in reefing sail. Not less than a thousand seamen, he says, fall from aloft, on American ships, every year, while in the discharge of their duty, and perish, unknelled, uncoffined, and unknown. He proceeds as follows:—

"Since the first of November last, one hundred and five seamen have been reported lost in this manner, on the homeward voyage of ships that have arrived in the port of New York alone. How many have been lost overboard, who were not reported, how many have fallen on the outward voyage, how many from ships arriving at other ports, how many from whalers and fishermen in distant seas, we have no means of ascertaining. Fifteen ships arriving here in the month of November, reported losing nineteen men from aloft. Eighteen ships arriving in December, reported twenty men. Seven ships arriving in January, reported seven men. Twelve ships arriving in February, reported eighteen men. Twelve ships arriving in March, reported twenty-three men. Fifteen ships arriving in April, reported sixteen men."

The article concludes with some very just remarks, in relation to the cause and the possibility of the prevention of this fearful mortality, confessing that *bad seamanship* has much to do with it.

Under the auspices of Andrew Jackson, an Act of Congress was passed, and approved March 2, 1837, providing a system of Apprenticeship for the Navy. During the last session of Congress, the Secretary of the Treasury, urged upon the Committee on Naval Affairs, some provisions to make this law effective. Of these apprentices, he says, that about sixty, each year, should be transferred to the Naval Academy. Those next in proficiency can become warrant officers, and the third grade can be made petty officers, and the remainder, sailors. This would open to apprentices, the highest honors of the naval service, and secure a better class of men. He says that but one-fifth are successful, under the present system, and the remainder leave the service. He credits the failure of the law of 1837 to the anomaly of educating boys for the naval service, without any promise of promotion. He expresses the belief, that this prejudice is fast passing away, and that upon the legislation proposed depends our prosperity and welfare.

A circular of the Navy Department, dated January 1, 1866, states that the department, having deemed it advisable to resume the enlistment of boys for the navy, to serve until they arrive at twenty-one years of age, unless sooner discharged, as authorized by Act of Congress, approved March 2, 1837, the following regulations have been adopted, for the purpose of effecting the object of the law, and will be observed accordingly.

The leading ideas of this system are to be found in the second, eighth, eighteenth, twenty-second, and twenty-eighth rules. A good English education, is a requisite for admission. Those admitted have a chance to compete for the three yearly appointments to the Naval Academy, and are also eligible as warrant officers. They are instructed in all the practical duties of a seaman, their whole time being devoted to that purpose. They are divided into three classes, paid eight, nine and ten dollars per month, one-tenth part of each lad's pay being retained until the close of his term of enlistment.

The wide range of social and industrial interests, which would be benefited by adoption of these views respecting instruction in the work of life, may be seen by a few extracts from respectable sources:—

"Monsieur Blot, who has been imparting to the women of New York some practical hints upon the proper mode of preparing meats and vegetables for the table, has been engaged by the Cooper Union of that city, to deliver, on four successive Saturday evenings, a series of lectures, illustrated by practical experiments, on cooking. The course is free to all, and the Cooper Institute, which is to be the *cuisene* of the occasion, will no doubt be crowded. If it is true, as has been stated, that M. Blot does not devote his attention to ragouts and fricassees, but descends to plain beefsteak, and mutton chops, the practical value of his lectures will be of incalculable advantage to those who attend. We wish the greatest success to M. Blot, and should his mission produce any good results in Gotham, we promise him a cordial welcome to 'the hub,' for it is a fact, that few will deny, that not one gentleman in a hundred, in this city, hazards a dinner party at his own home, to more than half a dozen intimate friends, fearful lest the meats or vegetables should tell of the inferiority of his cook.

"With the best market in the United States, if we can believe the recent report of the market committee of the city council, a large majority of our citizens, if they wished to entertain a stranger, would seek the club-house, or some one of our well-known public houses, in order to secure a well-cooked repast of either fish, flesh, or fowl."

A correspondent of the " Commercial Advertiser " gives some facts of interest in regard to the construction of German railroads:—

"Once on the road, we had leisure to see how excellent the German railroads are. The rails are smooth and straight, and not bent as with us by a poorly constructed and uneven railroad track. The joints are well held together by fastenings, and never bushy or bent at the ends. The ballast of the road is everywhere in complete order, and flush up on the outer side of the rail, and level with the ties, only just covering them in the middle. The track itself, neatly gravelled, is kept clean of grass including several feet beyond the rails, and the roads are, considering the drouth, very free from dust. The culverts and bridges are of the highest class, and our railroads, even the very best, are a disgrace compared with them in this particular. The same is true as to depots and their surroundings. It is clear that European railroad engineers would condemn every railroad in the United States as unsafe; for, according to their standard, we have really no railroads. The more I examine and inquire, and the more I become acquainted with the details, the more I feel ashamed as an American railroad man."

The weighty considerations of national existence ally themselves very closely with the adoption of these ideas, in military instruction. Are we willing to accept the condition of our country at the beginning of the war, as a proper or a necessary one? Do we not realize now that among the causes of the rebellion, and not the least of them, must be reckoned our unprepared situation. We observe the failure of all comprehensive militia systems; their ill success is intimately connected with our loose ideas in training, and our excessive devotion of time to labor and business. In our indifference to this aspect of public affairs we forget the essential weakness of a government which is unable to compel the obedience of the treasonable and disaffected.

The response of the legislature to the petition quoted at the beginning of this article may be found in chapter 270, Acts of 1865. The ancient penalty of imprisonment is repealed, and in its place, a bond in the sum of two hundred dollars or less substituted, mutually obligatory in its terms.

The advocates of this law, at the time of its enactment, felt obliged to concede that it was more prophetic than practical in its character, though it is understood that the city of Boston has, in some instances, adopted the principle involved.

The different hearings on the questions of labor have developed the fact that a considerable number of large establishments, in various parts of the State, have adopted the plan of a bonus or gratuity, to be given at the end of the term of service. Others reserve a portion of the wages, as we have seen is done by the government, in the case of the naval apprentices. These expedients have been, to say the least, hopeful in their results.

In connection with reduced hours, efficient aid may be expected from the trade organizations, as it is observable that those working the shortest time, as the hatters and some others, are the most successful in enforcing reasonable regulations in this respect. I have dwelt at some length on this theme of instruction in labor, because I conceive that public interest will be supported by public opinion in the event of a reduction, to obviate whatever there may be sacrificial in the reform by efficient customs, if not systems, of instruction.

Employers and employees agree in the belief that labor in some of its practical relations is deteriorating. Each party charges the blame upon the other. It seems quite certain that the interests of both will compel agreement on this question. The reduction to eight hours, for certain descriptions of labor, may be a measure imperatively called for by the claims of the intellectual and moral nature, irrespective of increased productiveness; but once introduced, it will be aided and enforced by the every-day needs of both parties.

Beecher says, "It may confidently be predicted, therefore, that if workmen have not leisure for self-culture, they can have it; and it may be just as confidently predicted that the employer will more than make up the diminution in time by the difference in the results of the labor. The thousand petty wastes that accompany ignorant, discontented work, compared with the savings of a man's thinking, willing work, amount to far more than the difference between eight hours and ten hours. But the work that is eight hours must be a much finer quality of steel than the work that is ten, or it will not bear the strain."

Relations of the Hours of Labor to the Farm.

The opposition of the farming interest to reduction of hours is a noticeable feature of the present agitation.

Mr. Wetherell, who appeared before the first commission in behalf of land-holding farmers, acknowledges that the rule for a day's work is fourteen hours for six months in the summer, or from sun to sun; meals, he says, will diminish it a little. Sometimes they begin before sunrise and work after it sets, (page 1, folio 2, Reports of Evidence.) That opposition must be regarded as equally directed against the reduction of time to ten hours, though inquiry shows that some farming of an amateur character in the neighborhood of our cities is done on the reduced time.

In this connection it is but fair to state, that the interests which press the question of the hours of labor, consider the position of the farmer working on his own property as identical with that of the master-workman, or his foreman, and propose no discussion as to the duration of labor under such circumstances. It may also be said in this admission, that if the labor of the trades could be carried on with the advantages of the farmer working on his own property, any agitation like the present would be not only unnecessary but impossible. Mr. Wetherell explains this well in his answer to Mr. Wyman. "The question is, whether a man working for himself would not be less exhausted doing the same work than if he worked for wages?" "I think that would be a fact whether he worked on a farm, or in a shop, or anywhere else. Arthur Young says, 'Give a man a barren rock and he will make a garden of it. Give him nine years' lease of a garden and he will make a desert of it.' Therefore I say, these farmers will endure much more working for themselves than if they were obliged to work for others. I thought of this when the testimony was given in regard to Indian Orchard. They account the toil over when they leave the factory. These people will go out of the factory weary, fagged out, yet they will work two or three hours with zest in the garden, or on the land about their premises, anything they can do to improve the place. This is not only on account of their using another set of muscles, but the interest they have in it. This brings me to another point I forgot to mention. It is this: that the farmer's work is unlike that of any shop or in-door work in this respect. No farmer can do the same kind of work during six months. The work is constantly changing. The same day he is employed in different kinds of work, calling into play different muscles and different degrees of interest."

In the discussion of this question in its relations to health and longevity, the farming population are generally considered as a unit, which is manifestly incorrect. The figures of the twenty-third registration report confirm the idea that, from some cause, there is a great disparity between the farmer and the farm-laborer. The 66th page, giving the ages at death of the occupations for the last twenty-one years in this State, rate the farmers at 64.16, and laborers of all trades, 46.07.

The point where there is a difference of opinion, and where inquiry is awakened, and interest excited, is in reference to the condition of youth, whether indented or otherwise, and the situation of hired labor on the farm. Intelligence and morals claim the candid consideration by the community of the question whether a continuous day's work of severe manual labor, from the rising of the sun to the going down thereof, by a laborer, presumed to have his own family and duties to attend to, can, in this age of the world, be upheld as just or necessary. The ground taken by the first commission, that " the udder of the cow, the shining of the sun in haying time, and the unforeseen contingencies of navigation," must forever bind the farmer and the seaman to indefinite prolongation of labor, seems to me untenable. The tide-workers of the docks, in the repairs of shipping, have adjusted themselves both to the ten and eight-hour changes in labor, and work without the slightest friction, in connection with both these systems; yet the tidal wave is the very emblem of irresistible power.

I find, in a valuable work entitled "Letters written in the Interior of Cuba" by the Rev. Abiel Abbot, of Beverly, the statement "that on the French sugar estates in the West Indies they work four hours at a time in turn, which makes the fatigue comparatively light." A detailed account in the same book of a sugar estate in Cuba, working four hundred and fifty slaves, states that "the proprietor carefully avoids overworking his negroes, as tending to fill his infirmary. In the winter he gives them a recess from labor at noon of an hour and a half, and in summer of three hours, and no night work is permitted on the estate. The best comment on these humane arrangements is, that a more healthy, muscular, active set of negroes, as many have remarked, is not to be found on the island."

At a meeting of planters in the State of Georgia, held November 24, 1864, to communicate to United States officials their views respecting colored labor, they state, in their second item, that they wish some mode of compelling laborers to perform *ten hours* of faithful labor in each twenty-four hours, Sundays excepted. (Document accompanying the Report of Gen. Carl Schurz, Ex. Doc., 39th Congress, 1st session.)

As seamen have been named in the same connection as the farming interest, some examination of their circumstances will be pertinent, and will reveal the fact that their condition does admit the application of a "fixed measure of time." R. H. Dana, Jr., in his personal narrative, "Two Years before the Mast," makes this detailed statement:—

"The crew are divided into two divisions, as equally as may be, called the watches. They divide the time between them, being on and off duty, as it is called, on deck and below, every other four hours. In a man-of-war, and in some merchantmen, this alternation of watches is kept up throughout the twenty-four hours; but our ship, like most merchantmen, had 'all hands' from twelve o'clock until dark, except in bad weather, when we had watch and watch.

"An explanation of the 'dog watches' may perhaps be of use to one who has never been at sea. They are to shift the watches each night, so that the same watch need not be on deck at the same hours. In order to effect this, the watch from four to eight P. M. is divided into two half or dog watches, one from four to six and the other from six to eight."

Close analysis of these hours will show that the seaman, in the usual routine of his life, is sure of six hours of daylight for himself, (except in bad weather ;) and in the case of men-of-war, and certain classes of merchantmen, where watch and watch is kept up, he has eight. Consideration of these hours in connection with those of miners makes it plain that they obviate three of the principal objections to the prevailing system.

First, the evil effects of monotonous employment, in connection with subdivided labor ; and, second, time by daylight, one of the greatest of blessings to the workman, is obtained. Third, the maximum of fatigue is so evenly adjusted to the leisure gained, that mental effort can be more readily exerted. The life of Henry Martyn, the English pioneer missionary to India, contains a statement happily illustrating this :—

"The subject of this memoir was born at Truro, in the county of Cornwall. His father was originally in a very humble situation of life, having been a laborer in the mines of Gwenap, the place of his nativity. With no education but such as a country reading-school afforded, he was compelled to engage, for his daily support, in an employment which, dreary and unhealthy as it was, offered some advantages, of which he most meritoriously availed himself. The miners, it seems, are in the habit of working and resting alternately every four hours; and the periods of relaxation from manual labor they frequently devote to mental improvement. In the intervals of cessation from toil, John Martyn acquired a complete knowledge of arithmetic, and also some acquaintance with mathematics; and no sooner had he gathered these valuable and substantial fruits of persevering diligence, in a soil most unfriendly to their growth, than he was raised from a state of poverty and depression to one of comparative ease and comfort. Being admitted to the office of Mr. Daniel, a merchant of Truro, he lived there as chief clerk very respectably, enjoying considerably more than a competency.

"It is further said of his son Henry, on entering college at Cambridge, that his decided superiority in mathematics soon appeared; and the highest academical honor, that of senior wrangler, was awarded to him in January, 1801, at which period he had not completed the twentieth year of his age."

Dr. Bartlett, of Chelmsford, in his letter to the first commission, has aptly stated the needs of the farming interest:—

"Such is now the desire for general reading and information, that if you can devise any means by which the farmer may be able to reduce his period of labor, you will do more for his solid education than all the agricultural colleges in the world."

I answer this question by saying, *that leisure will never come of its own accord. All that has been obtained, has been by effort, and is maintained by daily self-denial.* Official recognition, as an initiative for the sake of authoritative example, is regarded as essential. This we have seen was necessary for the trades. It will be still more so for the agricultural interest. If they are further willing to remedy the lack of social facilities of their laborers by a cordial co-operation with them in this work, it will advance to successful results. A theme so influential in its general bearings should have an unprejudiced examination. Reticence borders closely on indifference to human welfare. The agricultural literature of the day indicates new developments of the greatest moment, in whose solution this question has claims for a more candid discussion than it has received. I have thought best to make here a special allusion to the

MOTIVES, WAYS AND MEANS, AND BENEFITS OF REDUCTION IN THE TRADES.

Thirty years since, the workmen of the heavy trades came to the conclusion that every intelligent human being had responsibilities and privileges which could not by any possibility be fulfilled in a course of life occupied by the three conditions of labor, nutrition and sleep. As a result of this conclusion, agitation ensued. By executive authority, a new measure of time for a day's labor was inaugurated. At first so specific in its application, as to be open to narrow criticism on the score of partiality, it has proved prolifically germinal; and, with more or less of directness, has affected every interest of society.

During the discussion, it was said that the masses could never be brought to adhere to a day of labor which cut them off from two or more hours of employment. Experience has demonstrated the contrary, and multitudes of workmen who calculate closely, know that the short hours are compensated to the individual and to society.

The most prominent facts, conditions and results of the amelioration in time, may be briefly stated thus:—

Greater relative vigor of the workman, in connection with the imperative obligation to reduce time from the exhausted portion of the day. Less loss of time in consequence of a sensible relief in the daily duration of labor. Greater healthfulness, especially during the summer season. A quicker return to labor, and a more rapid recovery of strength after sickness. The increased respectability of labor, which retains many in production. An approximate equalization of the day's work, which has largely contributed to diffuse employment over the year, and thus diminished distress during the winter season. Multiplied inventions, subdivisions in trades, and, generally, a more intellectual and progressive impetus to production. Openings for the industrial classes in evening exercises of a religious, reformatory, political and miscellaneous character. The noticeably increased influence of woman, closely connected with the fact that the home has gained time formerly devoted to the shop or counting-room. In connection with railroads, it has aided the growth of suburban towns and cities; thus sensibly relieving, and even turning into a blessing, one of the most remarkable, and, in some respects, most injurious results of modern society,—the growth of large cities. The popular mind has been sensibly impressed with a conviction that social progress is connected with our institutions. Under these influences, the masses of the North have borne hopefully the burdens of the war, and have been met in a similar intelligent spirit of sacrifice by the operative classes of England; both descriptions of labor being inspired by the elevating influences of recent reductions. These advantages have been gained in spite of the depressing effect of foreign labor, the rapid increase of which has been brought about mainly by other causes.

In the light of this experience, is it reasonable to suppose that Massachusetts would be the loser by giving her youth in the country and her farm laborers from one to three hours at noon, according to the season of the year. Page 28, Report of the first Commission states, that the probable present value of the farms of the whole country is ten billions of dollars, and in connection with this, argues against reduction; but if it were twenty, it would only make the daily neglect or violation of any of the primary elements of human development the more disastrous.

By the difference between the number of farms returned on page 760, Massachusetts Industrial Returns of 1865, and the number of those employed in farming, there would seem to be nearly 24,000 laborers' and farmers' sons in the State, whose interests and well-being are involved in this question.

Will Leisure be Wisely Used?

Deliberate consideration of this point, impresses me with the conviction that the people may be relied upon for such use of time as will eventuate in good.

Even if it be admitted that the lower element of labor would not at first employ it in the wisest manner, the experience of America in reductions shows the most prominent tendency to be local expansion, embracing, as we have seen, comprehensive influences of an elevating nature.

A strong presumption in the direction of liberal views, may be inferred from the fact that liabilities to abuse of leisure have been disregarded by the Divine Being, in the institution of the Sabbath. There seems to be sufficient reason for believing that ampler conditions of leisure than those prevailing at present are absolutely necessary for the further development of the industrial portion of the community. Under the present providential arrangements, no provision is made by revelation for the claims of the intellect, or the culture, apart from religion, of the finer sensibilities.

"Remember the Sabbath day to keep it holy," is a command which no relaxation of rigid observance can with propriety entirely abrogate.

The Old Testament has, however, a very strong intimation, that a national provision for leisure on the grandest scale, comports with general prosperity, with the essential needs of human nature, and with the divine plans for the well-being of mankind.—(25th chapter of Leviticus.)

1. And the Lord spake unto Moses in Mount Sinai, saying,
2. Speak unto the children of Israel, and say unto them, When ye come unto the land which I give you, then shall the land keep a sabbath unto the Lord.
3. Six years thou shalt sow thy field, and six years thou shalt prune thy vineyard, and gather in the fruit thereof;
4. But in the seventh year shall be a sabbath of rest unto the land, a sabbath for the Lord: thou shalt neither sow thy field, nor prune thy vineyard.
5. That which groweth of its own accord of thy harvest thou shalt not reap, neither gather the grapes of thy vine undressed: for it is a year of rest unto the land.
6. And the sabbath of the land shall be meat for you; for thee, and for thy servant, and for thy maid and for thy hired servant, and for thy stranger that sojourneth with thee.
20. And if ye shall say, What shall we eat the seventh year? behold, we shall not sow nor gather in our increase:
21. Then will I command my blessing upon you in the sixth year, and it shall bring forth fruit for three years.

Reference to the twenty-third chapter, verses twenty-third to twenty-fifth inclusive, the thirty-sixth verse, as also the thirty-ninth and fortieth, will show additional provisions of the same character, evidently intended to equalize the blessings of leisure over the intervening years. The Sabbatic year would hardly have been ordained, and its powerful influences thrown across the path of continued application to labor and to gain, if the moral exposures of leisure were so great as some interests among us seem to fear.

We have now a perfect religion,—the full and complete expression of the divine will, in all matters pertaining to moral and spiritual interests; and, in connection with the gospel, the freest government yet instituted, insures those upward tendencies which characterize the masses of the North.

Defective institutions in a portion of our country have degraded labor in the popular estimation; but the evils which followed in the train of slavery, were not the result of a suitable amount of daily leisure, but of idleness.

It has been prominently remarked in this direction, that "this eight hour movement has a train of seductive graces in its wake, intellectual culture, refined leisure, moral recreation, domestic felicity, political intelligence and public virtue. All these are prominently put forward as attainable results, if this desideratum is adopted. Are there not men of evil propensities who will use the additional leisure as far in other ways? Do none of the working men drink? have none of them other bad habits? Are we quite sure that your great remedy would be an unmixed good. Because, if it be true that such grand results are to be achieved by leisure, how very easy it would be to reform the world."

This forcible critique is uncharitable in its verdict, as but few will contend that a reform of such a decided character can be introduced without some exposure, sacrifice and delay in its results. Its principal defect lies in the direction of our present point. It assumes, impliedly at least, that those conditions of leisure and relief from manual labor which, among the trading and professional classes have resulted in refinement and elevation of character, will, to a great extent fail, when applied to the laboring masses. The events of the present day have in a surprising manner revealed the character and tendencies of the common people of this country, and they have borne the test in a way which ought to inspire confidence in their judgment and morals. The following summary of facts is too conclusive to admit of reputation.

The London "Times" of December 15, 1863, has an extract from a letter of its Richmond correspondent, which makes the following remarkable admission:—

"No one, who has been conversant with the Northern States during the last two and a half years, can have failed to notice with astonishment the faith, stronger than death, which the Northerners have exhibited in their manifest Destiny, *their Religion*, their Alpha and Omega,—their dream of dominion from sea to sea, and, to quote Mr. Everett's own words, 'from the icy pole to the flaming belt of the equator.' The successes of the South have altogether failed to inspire them with a tithe of that confidence in themselves which neither defeat, nor hope deferred, nor illusions dispelled, have ever shaken out of the Northerners. Deny it who may, there is something sublime in this shadowy earnestness and misty magnificence of Northern faith and self-reliance."

To give its full value to this acknowledgment, thus extorted from the bitterest hate, it should be remembered that it was penned a year and a half before the end of the war, at a time when the revelation of national character which it verifies, had not been proved by the horrors of Andersonville, or the concluding campaign of Grant. Should we not, in estimating its worth, also bear in mind the character of the issues presented to the people in the memorable presidential election of 1864? They were free to choose which of two courses they would take. One, appealing to the infirmities and selfishness of our nature, led to a shameful peace. The other was invested with the repulsive features of Golgotha; but it was taken without hesitation, and, as we judge, in a spirit of moral and intellectual heroism which is full of promise for the future of the masses of the American people.

If we consider the character of the freedmen from an enlarged view, we find the same encouraging aspects. Are they willingly sunk in ignorance?

The South, all through the war, has been vocal with the elementary sounds of the English tongue, to a great extent dropping from the lips of those far advanced in life. But as morals, not mind, will mainly control the decision of this question, we are led to the record of their deeds during their hour of trial.

We all thought—even the South apprehended at the beginning—that the long-continued wrongs of slavery would be avenged in insurrection and murder; and when this prediction failed, we charged it to their debasement, little dreaming that in two years we should ask from them, and that not in vain, for the exercise of the sturdiest qualities of manhood to aid us in our desperate struggle.

By self-restraint under unparalleled suffering, and energetic action at the moment suggested by the highest wisdom, Labor, in its deepest humiliation, has developed the most sterling qualities.

It will be said, we concede that American workingmen would, as a body, use the time well; but the foreign element is too much depressed to need or to improve by the change. Waiving the consideration of the point, whether or no more time for the masses is not an elementary condition of their elevation, we will allow our thoughts to cross the ocean, to the homes of those who form one large source of supply to our laboring population—the operatives of Lancashire. Their course is too well known to require any notice beyond the following suggestive extract from a speech at Rochdale:—

"The masses of England have never flinched since the war begun from their duty, but have sympathized with the North from first to last. We, the people, rather than meddle a hair's-breadth to turn the scale against them, have borne untold miseries and uncounted losses."

The lot of a portion of them, it is true, has been one of profound depression, yet it is plain that they feel for good the impulse of our institutions. How industrious they are; their savings already give them influence as a class. If they do not make the wisest use of time at present, is it not mainly due to extremes of labor and the occasional excesses of holidays? The leisure which is proposed is in its conditions guarded from these exposures.

In view of such developments, why distrust the industrial masses? One remarkable aspect of Divine Revelation favors liberality in opinion on this question: that is, that the poor, as a distinct class, are never denounced in the Scriptures, while its most earnest and solemn warnings are uttered to the rich.

Two avenues of progress, parallel, yet for much of their course remote from each other, seem to me to confine within their respective bounds the different interests of society. They often approach, and tend, more and more, as knowledge increases, to abandon their isolation, and unite all differences, or modifications of opinion, feeling or interest, in one ample and harmonious onward movement.

Mill gives the characteristics of one of these columns in his Treatise on Liberty, page 25:—

"It is proper to state that I forego any advantage which could be derived to my argument, from the idea of abstract right, as a thing independent of utility. I regard utility as the ultimate appeal in all ethical questions; but it must be utility in the largest sense, grounded on the permanent interests of man as a progressive being."

Guizot reveals the other on pages 114 and 137 of "The History of Civilization":—

"This fact is evident: the intellectual and moral progress of Europe has been essentially theological." "Every question that has been started, whether philosophical, political, or historical, has been considered in a religious point of view."

Into the latter division of the elements which contend with each other in moulding the institutions of our country, the great mass of laborers, by influences more or less direct, must be held to belong. It was not utility, but right, which held the starving weavers of Lancashire to their course in the cotton famine, and influenced the soldiers of our army to loyalty at Andersonville, in spite of the most seductive offers,—nor can we suppose philosophic considerations to have controlled the colored population of the South. Religious knowledge, widely diffused, had laid the foundations for practical results. Defective and inconsistent their piety may have been, but it has been sufficient to save a continent from a repetition of the scenes of St. Domingo.

But while I thus contend for the general rectitude of the masses, considered as a whole, and with proper allowance for experience to correct mistakes and errors, I am ready to acknowledge that there is a profound sense in which it is true that social advancement is due to the influence of minorities. The dawn of history reveals this fact in the promise to Abraham, that if ten righteous men could be found in the doomed city, it should be spared for their sake. God's judgments are not arbitrary, but righteous altogether. The saving of a city has sometimes depended on fewer than ten, and, in the broad conditions of redemption, divine ministrations give place to a minority of mortals in the intentions of mercy to our race. Our intimate association, the common infirmities of our nature, the dread exposures of mortality, and the profound sympathies of humanity, impart to an enlightened individual, or to a number of such, powers peculiar in their nature, powers which could not be exercised by a higher order of beings. To a certain extent, the same conditions apply to the relations which exist between the extremes of society. One of the most noticeable hindrances to the elevation of the masses, as such, has been found to be the fact that they have had no leaders. " Manual labor has to a very great extent made a dividing line in society." All developments in morals or ability have taken their possessors away from their brethren in toil, and, to a great extent, limited that power for good which comes from parity of circumstances. Moral efforts among seamen are painfully embarrassed by the immediate desertion of their calling by reformed men. The unparalleled increase of corporate and concentrated employ has tended to obliterate this line, by confining a more intelligent class than formerly to the position of employees, interposing, as it has, insuperable obstacles to their independent control of business. Parties the most decided in their opposition to reductions agree in admitting the existence of this class, and concede its straitened situation; but it has not been so apparent to many that to this interest, more than to any other, will society be indebted for safety and improvement in the future.

The Rev. William Arthur, an English clergyman of reputation, says: —

"Another point of view would be this: give us the half holiday, and you would throw into the recreations of our working people numbers of the best and noblest of the workingmen; men who will not run into diversions upon the Lord's day, and, therefore, leave the diversions of the people who do take them upon that day without the tone and elevation and moral influence which the best of their own class would give them if they were in the midst of them; but give them half the working day, and you will find that your most intelligent, religious and valuable workingmen will take their proper standing, and exercise their proper influence upon the recreations which are resorted to by their fellow workmen."

The economic spirit of the age fails in its solution of this question of reduction of hours, mainly because it cannot see where high moral truths connect with every day affairs. The ten-hour workman sacrifices every summer day two or three hours to uses more elevated than those of production. In this self-denial, in the success of his movement, in the fact that all but an exceptional class hasten to the suburban home, in preference to the drinking saloon of the city, he bases his claim upon society for a completion of the work so well begun.

But the cultured and monetary interests of society stumble at this point. They assume the present routine to be a wise and righteous one. In the interests, as they sincerely suppose, of the productive class, they contest reductions. Contrary to uniform experience, the operative is made to believe that his pay will be permanently lowered. Efforts are used to hinder by hourly wages the orderly tendency of the human mind, to crystallize around a certain length of time, as a suitable limit for a day of labor. The cry is uttered, with evident sincerity, " Foreign competition will ruin us!" and yet, in spite of these objections and numerous defeats, and without the injurious results predicted, the mass of uneducated and isolated laborers are steadily lessening the duration of toil. The spectacle is so singular, yet so sublime, that it can only be compared with the slow but ceaseless motion of an iceberg, every foot of whose progress is vehemently opposed by the superficial forces of winds, waves and currents, but whose base, reaching down a thousand feet, takes hold of motive powers, hidden from the eye, but irresistible in their power.

Impressed with the conviction that these developments are in harmony with the Divine will, thoughtful workingmen relieve themselves of the apprehension that they will suffer in their material interests by further devotion of time to higher avocations.

They do not doubt that the true course in the present crisis lies in the direction of such new customs of labor as will favor a culture of heart and brain, ending in the development of new productive powers, and in a more equal division of the results of forces, already operative.

In philosophic terms, the principles which in this aspect of the question lead to these conclusions, are defined by De Tocqueville, in chapter 16, 2d volume "Democracy in America" : —

"There is a closer tie than is commonly supposed between the improvement of the soul and the amelioration of what belongs to the body. Man may leave these two things apart, and consider each of them alternately, but he cannot sever them entirely without at last losing sight of both.

"The beasts have the same senses as ourselves, and very nearly the same appetites. We have no sensual passions which are not common to our race and theirs, and which are not to be found, at least in the germ, in a dog as well as in a man. Whence is it, then, that the animals can only provide for their first and lowest wants, whereas we can infinitely vary and endlessly increase our enjoyments?

"We are superior to the beasts in this, that we use our souls to find out those material benefits to which they are only led by instinct. In man, the angel teaches the brute the art of satisfying its desires. It is because man is capable of rising above the things of the body, and of contemning life itself, of which the beasts have not the least notion, that he can multiply these same goods of the body to a degree which the inferior races cannot conceive of.

"Whatever elevates, enlarges and expands the soul, renders it more capable of succeeding in those very enterprises which concern it not. Whatever, on the other hand, enervates or lowers it, weakens it for all purposes, the chief as well as the least, and threatens to render it almost equally impotent for both. Hence the soul must remain great and strong, though it were only to devote its strength and greatness from time to time to the service of the body. If men were ever to content themselves with material objects, it is probable that they would lose by degrees the art of producing them; and they would enjoy them in the end, like the brutes, without discernment and without improvement."

THE RELATIONS OF THE DIFFERENT DESCRIPTIONS OF LABOR TO EACH OTHER, TO THE GROWTH OF CITIES, TO THE SOCIAL, EDUCATIONAL AND SANITARY CONDITION OF THE INDUSTRIAL CLASSES.

Reference to the Journal of the House of 1866, will show that the vote in favor of an eight-hour labor, was thrown almost entirely by gentlemen representing municipal or suburban constituencies. I propose to use this fact in its representative character, and discuss its connections.

The Memorial of the Boston Sanitary Association, House Document 112, 1861, page 26, gives the following figures:—

In the twenty years from 1840 to 1860, twenty-eight large cities and towns in Massachusetts, gained . . 145 per cent.
The rest of the State gained . . . . 32 "
Fifty-nine largest cities in the U. S. gained . . 198 "
The rest of the United States gained . . 75 "

Recent summaries of statistics indicate increasing tendencies in this direction, since the war concluded. Seen from the point of our inquiry, the motives which aid in producing these results, may be found in the necessities of laborers. Bound by no tie of business interest to any particular locality, workmen and operatives, as classes, are unwilling to purchase a house, or even to settle in any small place, where they are limited in their choice of employers. They understand instinctively, that permanency in this respect, means reduced wages, and in all but the most liberal employ, a limitation of the liberty of action, so sweet to the human mind. The principles involved are of general application. Essex thrives in the construction of schooners for the fishing towns. Distribute her builders among the various ports where that interest is located, and their prosperity would cease. The general desire for the introduction of business into a town, would not affect the course of a party desiring to have a vessel built. The inward thought would be, you are dependent on this place for a living; you have bought your house and ship-yard; you have shut yourself out from the general demand, and if you build my vessel, it must be at the minimum price. Any successful system of co-operation in manufactures; of partnerships of labor and capital, or any means by which the industrial classes can be made sharers in the profits of labor, will operate to fix the residence of the workman, and, in connection with the local expression of reduced hours, to decide its healthfulness, and counteract the tendencies to centralization.

Still keeping within the limits of our inquiry, I find that the conditions of farm work force the sons of our yeomanry into the city, and tend to diminish the production of food, by limiting the supply of labor, and lowering its character.

An able article, by Mrs. L. B. Harris, of Detroit, on this point, may be found in the U. S. Agricultural Report of 1863, page 307. She begins with saying:—

"No fact is more evident among farming communities, than that the boys almost universally grow up with a distaste for farm pursuits."

To which I will add, that no peculiarity in the views or feelings of the masses, in our cities, is more marked, than an inbred hatred of farm labor, turning mainly on the length of its hours, and the violence done by them, to the physical immaturity and hopeful aspirations of youth.

The extreme depression of a portion of our emigrant population, in connection with circumstances which I shall allude to, controls the residence of large numbers in our cities, with results sufficiently impressive to engage the attention of professional and philanthropic men.

The material and moral consequences of this strange agglomeration, developed clearly in the account of the meeting of the Fourth National Sanitary Convention, in Boston, June 1860. Dr. Ordronaux introduced to the convention, Mr. Samuel B. Halliday, of New York, as a gentleman having a speciality for the exploration, night and day, of the purlieus of city life, and the collection of statistical embodiments of those observations.

Mr. Halliday, after some preliminary remarks, proceeded to say, (page 59) :—

"I am sorry, sir, that Boston, in some particulars, is so much like New York. Within two minutes' walk of this beautiful hall, where we are to-day, Boston rivals the Five Points. I am sorry it is so. I have here, sir, in four columns of foolscap, the census of a single house, but a few squares from the place where we are met, containing apartments for seventy-four families. I have the age of every man, woman and child in those seventy-four families. I have also the number of deaths of children that have occurred in those families, with the ages of those children at the time of their deaths. I have also the number of stillbirths that have occurred in those families. The whole establishment, sir, is equivalent to our 'Barracks,' on Cherry Street, in New York, a spot which we regard as one of the worst possible in our city. Everything about that building, sir, is abominable. There is not an apartment in it, that by any possibility can ever be ventilated. The bed-rooms in which those families sleep, are entirely excluded from the light and air, except as these are admitted by a single door into the bed-room. The water-closets of that place, the gentlemen of Boston would not turn their dogs or pigs into. And these are the conditions of the life of human beings in our great cities of New York and Boston.

"This is not a question of local interest; large communities abound throughout the length and breadth of our land, and they are to continue, and will constantly increase in their denseness.

"The poor must live in our large cities. They must, from necessity, stay with us. They cannot pay even a five cent railroad fare, to ride to the better portion of those cities. The fare to and from their places of employment, would eat up one-third of their earnings, and the cost of transportation, some thirty-five dollars a year, would be more than one-half of what they pay for their rent. Seventy-five cents a week, was a very common price for the tenements in the building to which I allude; in some others, a dollar. The rental of this building is about $4,500 a year; the man who hires it pays $3,000 a year, and sub-lets it."

Dr. Curtis, of Boston, a portion of whose remarks I will give, says:—

"I am compelled to admit, that the building referred to is not the worst place we have in the city of Boston. But the matter has been brought so many times, in various ways, to the attention of the public authorities, and oftentimes before the government of our city, that it seems very discouraging indeed, for those who have labored long in this matter, that so little can be done. Why, sir! investigations of this nature, have brought to light facts, which present the municipal governments of our various cities as displaying an apathy, in this regard, very remarkable; and not to be accounted for. The number of premature deaths, and the extent of unnecessary disease which exists, in a financial point of view, or more in a moral aspect, cannot very well be exaggerated. I will state that a report upon the mortality of Boston, according to the census of 1855, showed the deaths in contiguous wards, was as twenty-three, to twelve."

Mr. Baily, of Boston, continued the debate, showing, by practical statements, page 62, the offensive condition of the outlets of the sewers.

"We have now only water-closets, and very few vaults; everything goes into our sewers. As the tide flows out from the flats, the deposits are left; miasma arises; sickness and death are the result."

Dr. S. L. Condict, of New Jersey, continued :—

"We have sewers laid upon an almost dead level; the inevitable consequence is, that they fill up, and become a source of disease and pestilence to the whole community. The subject has been often presented to our civil authorities, *and they dare not go in advance of public sentiment. And as a general rule, civil authorities will never go in advance of public sentiment, and public sentiment will never progress until it is enlightened.*"

The following letter, will show how much probability there is, of the mass of the people becoming sufficiently enlightened under present circumstances, to support by their votes, the authorities in such measures:—

MEDFORD, Mass., September 3, 1866.
To the Commission on the Hours of Labor.

GENTLEMEN:—I am a joiner, my work is mostly in Charlestown, Boston, East Boston, &c. I have to be up and stirring at 5 A. M., to get my breakfast. Take the cars at 6.25, get to my work at 7 A. M. and 1 P. M., leave work at 6, get home at 7, finish supper at $7\frac{1}{2}$ P. M. Am then generally too tired to do anything, or to read, and have to go to bed to get rest, and to be able to work next day. And thus my time goes.

Where is my time for reading and study? A little while in the cars, a few minutes at noon, and Sundays; blessed day of rest to a laboring man. *My case is like very many that I know.* I honestly ask for eight hours as a legal day's work. With much respect, yours.

In the solution of this social problem, labor asks a candid hearing. She says that our deliverance is to be found in the prevalence of those ideas, customs, institutions and habits, and those developments of character, which can only come through moderation of our excessive toil. She says, give us eight hours for the labor of the city, with such ameliorations of the hours of the farm and the mill as to bring them within the scope of the elevating influences of reductions; and it will soon be seen that the problem admits of an approximate solution.

The physical and moral conditions which tend to favorable results, may be suggestively indicated by beginning with agricultural labor. In a circle broken only by Massachusetts Bay, and mostly within twenty-five miles of Boston, a description of farming industry is found, which amounts, in round numbers, in five counties within those limits, to $700,000 per annum. (Statistics of market gardens, Industry of Massachusetts, 1865, p. 766.) It is a business apparently admitting of indefinite extension. The condition of its labor, and the mutual relations of the farm and the city, in this respect, may be seen in the following evidence.

Hours of Labor on the Market Farm of ——— ———, in the vicinity of Boston.

"Rise at $\frac{1}{4}$ to $\frac{1}{2}$ past 4, attend to horses and light work, breakfast at 5, get to work at $\frac{1}{2}$ past 5, dinner, 11, recess $\frac{1}{2}$ hour for dinner, supper at 5, about ½ hour, leave work at sunset, attend to chores after that. Making 14 hours of labor during the summer, outside of meals."

The young man who gave this information, is competent, by his intelligence, to fill a high position. He states these hours to be the rule for that class of farms, in the vicinity of Boston, and also that the men are not generally dissatisfied, because they mostly come from remote parts, the Provinces, &c., where they work as long hours, for less pay. He further states, that his employer is an intelligent, fair-minded man, who would like to shorten hours, but fears competition.

In another case, ——— ———, a lad of sixteen years, wishing employ, went on to a market farm for the season; was employed so incessantly and laboriously that he could not stand it, though strong and accustomed to labor; was often employed longer hours than those named in the previous item. When he left, his employer told him that it was a loss to him (the employer) of thirty dollars.

In commenting on these conditions of labor, the most noticeable error, which, I observe, is the statement of Mr. Halliday, as to the expense of getting out of the city. He says, " they cannot pay a five-cent car fare to ride to the better portion of the city." This may be true, but it does not seem to be the reason why they do not do it. That is to be found partly in the fact that there is not enough difference in the rent in healthier localities in the city to make it pay; and partly, also, that " barracks " can be more readily obtained to let to such tenants in localities remote from the advantages demanded by intelligent families. Less social odium is incurred by the parties leasing buildings for such purposes than would be the case if they should locate them in the " better portion " of the city.

But his statement is wrong in fact. It costs only six cents a day, or eighteen dollars a year, and four cents a day, or twelve dollars a year, for egress to the ample spaces of Chelsea, and East Boston, while South Boston and Dorchester can be reached by walking; and this expense would be more than met by the difference between the rents of Boston, and the localities named.

Having shown that the lack of money need not confine this class to the city, I will endeavor to state the remoter issues involved in the situation.

The following item from an able newspaper article, develops some of the traits of character of these classes:—

"The great cities are crowded with the improvident, the poor, and the sick, while work awaits them at various points with sure remuneration; and yet it is very seldom that even the promise of better things can tempt any of this class away from their crowded tenements into the purer air, and upon the cheaper lands of the country. The poorer Irish laborers are particularly gregarious in habit. In the country they are lonesome and discontented, and it is a very difficult thing to induce family servants or help to work anywhere but in the city."

Consider in this light the hours that I have shown as ruling on the farm in the vicinity of the city, and see what object it is for any of these people to leave permanently their crowded quarters. But few of them are single; their wives and children must be carried with them, or they will not go, at least, to stop any length of time. In the city they get ten hours, giving them a brief period at morning and night to be with their families. In the country every moment of daylight is grudged to them. The comparison must be sufficiently evident to effectually impress even their dull sensibilities with aversion. The transitory and insufficient supply of farm labor, and the remoteness of its source, is the natural result of these conditions. Whatever may be said of some localities, and some kinds of farming, it is believed that benefits of a remunerative character would follow reduction in this department as readily as they have been seen to do in the instances of the operative and handicraft vocations.

Looking still further, we should find that most of them were only needed in the summer. Now and then, some one more thrifty or fortunate than the rest, builds a small place in the country and remains; but as a class they are not wanted, or at least their presence is not desirable beyond the pressing wants of the hour. No provision in the interests of the farmer is made to take them out of the gripe of city landlords by the erection of such cottages as might meet their wants. The wise forecast of the mills and railroads, in this respect, is evident throughout the State.

Turning city-ward again, a close scrutiny of the habits of our American working-classes will show that in spite of their intelligent appreciation of the advantages of the suburbs, they are at present barely able to reach them. Boston dismissed, fourteen years ago, forty-two thousand of her business men and artisans every evening to her environs. The length of the day, counting the time from leaving home until the return, approximates the former hours, now admitted to have been excessive. In these circumstances, the labor of the city may be divided into three classes. A large portion of the foreign born, worked to excess by energetic and often unscrupulous overseers, subcontractors, etc., finds its home in the nearest alley. The same lack of self-respect which prevents it from claiming its rights in labor, exercises a leading influence in the choice, or rather lack of choice, of a home.

A considerable element of the better portion of the foreign population remains in decent, if not respectable, quarters in the city, while nearly the whole American working population are found in the suburbs; cheapness of rent ostensibly, pride of character really, the motive-power which brought them out of the city. If we follow them into their homes, we shall find that as a rule they are exhausted, and that it is only the most youthful and energetic that are available for public or social duties. The hurried reading of a cheap paper is the limit of intellectual exercise to the most of them. None but those possessing a superabundance of the most active qualities of our nature can bestir themselves, cleanse thoroughly, and make that change in dress which is required to feel at ease, or to be acceptable in good society.

One element of this employ, demands by every motive of elevated obligation fuller consideration than it has received. This is the class of females employed in shops, in sewing, and in various descriptions of manufacture. Mostly of American origin, necessitated to board either with or near their connections in the suburbs, held to ten hours through the year, much of their work quite exhausting, their condition as they enter their homes as late as seven, during the heats of summer or the driving storms of winter, cannot be reckoned any special honor to our civilization. Inquiry has satisfied me that their claim to a radical reduction is as good as any class of labor in the State.

The acknowledged intelligence of the American masses, whenever it can be brought to bear any given subject, fails in such questions as the sanitary conditions of cities, because the issue involves connections too extended for them to master in their present circumstances. It behooves that an evil must develop itself to a commanding magnitude, as slavery and the war did, before interest can be excited and the true aspects of the matter seen, so as to fortify the civil authorities by the vote of the masses. The " remarkable apathy not to be accounted for," which Doctor Curtis mentions, finds its true solution in the fact *that the destinies of this country are in the hands of its working classes; and they have not as yet attained a system of labor which admits of the performance of its high duties.*

I cannot but quote in this connection, the opinion founded on the experience of a life-time of the veteran in social reform, Lord Brougham :—

"If this bill (the ten-hours factory bill,) was framed to afford the opportunity of moral instruction and education to adults, it did not go far enough, and this the consistent advocates of short-time legislation had acknowledged when they demanded a reduction to eight hours. Every one knows that a man after ten hours toil, was too much fatigued to think of anything but rest and relaxation, and above all he was most in want of 'tired Nature's sweet restorer, balmy sleep.' He had been trying to educate the laboring man for forty years, and his constant competitor and antagonist, by which he had always been defeated, was Sleep."

To argue the point still further, it is contended that questions of such magnitude and universality of interest, hinging so directly in a part of their discussion on the question of the hours of labor, can never be properly settled until laboring men themselves have an influential hearing in their adjustment.

In the vote which I have alluded to at the beginning of this article, they have expressed themselves as nearly as the circumstances permit, true to those simultaneous movings of the masses, which are as extraordinary in their character as the instincts of the beaver or the bee.

It is evident that the American population has but just escaped the lowering influences of city residence. When they first agitated for ten hours, the railway system was unthought of, the time that it was then proposed to use directly for elevated purposes has been diverted to travel. *In urging eight hours they are simply carrying out their first intention, and success must liberate the respectable portion of labor from the same bondage, so far as time is concerned, which prompted the first movement.* This interest in society would then be felt in social questions as it is in politics, as an influential power on subjects now beyond its circumstances to grasp, while the shortened hours would tell immediately upon the depressed classes by a location which would bring them under the control of sanitary and refining influences. Give them a chance to get away by the same hours which the heavy trades are struggling for, under similar circumstances of excessive fatigue, and then if they do not move voluntarily; in the interests of human life, compel them. Are not the motives to this course of as great weight as those which have recently relieved Fort Hill of its population and placed it at the disposal of commerce ? A comprehensive view of the report of the Sanitary Convention compels me to the conviction, that the adoption of eight hours as the usual limit of a day's employ for the descriptions of labor which centre in the cities, will prove itself one of those " simple changes in physical life," mentioned by Guizot, " as having a powerful effect on the course of civilization."

The social condition of the European and Asiatic masses who are swarming our Atlantic and Pacific slopes, is ominous of of danger to our institutions. The remarkable fulfilment thus far of the prediction of a hundred million of inhabitants for the United States of nineteen hundred, should be a warning to us that apprehension on this subject is not premature. The remedial effects of our vast territory seems to be overestimated; it mitigates and postpones without removing the danger. The settlement of our frontier, however sparsely, raises the price of land beyond the means of a large portion of these classes to purchase, and Chicago and St. Louis contain, to-day, as much of poverty and suffering as our oldest cities.

RELATIONS OF THE HOURS OF LABOR TO WAGES.

The first promptings of nature are usually either defective in principle or erroneous in morals. The customs of daily life need occasional revision, to harmonize them with the conditions of society when inspired by free institutions.

Ideas have reversed impulses in commerce. Franklin's maxims have become obsolete in the counting-room, and, if regarded at all, are interpreted and applied as he would present them if living. It was the former mercantile practice to obtain the highest percentage of profit possible; the mature conclusion is, to increase the amount of profit by diminishing the percentage, thus enlarging the demand, and in so doing, repeating the profitable use of capital and relatively diminishing expenses. Recurrence to the old ideas, with the present experience, would compare in wisdom with the course of the green-hand who declined to ship on the whaleman for a lay of one barrel in every one hundred and sixty-five, but concluded an arrangement for one in every one hundred and seventy-five; deceived by the first impressions of numeric magnitude.

A similar fallacy prevails extensively respecting the wages and productive results of labor; because it is true that an individual workman can earn more in a single day of twelve hours than in one of ten, it is argued, or rather the conclusion is taken for granted, that a reduction from ten to eight hours will entail a loss of one-fifth in wages, or its equivalent, a rise of one-fifth in prices, with the further certainty of a reduction of one-fifth of the products of the country. These ideas have been disproved, so far as experience of the results of the first reduction can be depended upon to guide us in foretelling the future. Two laboring populations, as wide apart as the poles in their circumstances, the operatives of England and the heavy trades of the United States, have successfully shown that relief, pecuniary or otherwise, from the narrow conditions of uncultivated labor, is not to be found in an increase of its hours.

The citizens' circular of the present Commission proposes as its fourth question—" Was any deduction made in wages when the ten-hour system was introduced?" The uniform answer has been in the negative. The responses have been sufficiently numerous to cover all classes of mechanical employ in the eastern section of the State. Evidence has been developed in the answers to this question, showing that a strenuous effort was made to prevent the establishment of ten hours as a unit, by insisting on twelve hours,—but paying, for at least one season, twelve-tenths of the market price for a day's work, in a neighborhood where the new rule had been generally accepted without a reduction of wages.

If there was any rise in prices of commodities, it would be apt to show in the manufacture where the shorter day first came in use. This was in ship-building. The revolution in that business has been such as to render it impossible to tell by the price of large vessels, whether any increase took place. At the time the day was shortened, the size of ships was increasing, very few being built afterwards of less than a thousand tons, the former maximum having been six hundred tons. At the same time, the material of construction was changed from oak to the cheaper southern pine. These alterations so affect the prices as to make it impossible to institute a comparison of them in a series of years before or after the change. There is but one description of vessel which has continued to be built of the same size and material as formerly. These are the schooners engaged in the cod and mackerel fishery, forming usually an important element in the industrial returns from Essex County.

There are no public records by which the price of these vessels can be ascertained; but personal inquiry has given me the dates and prices of some fifteen vessels, covering the period from 1830 to 1850:—

1830,	$24 00 per ton.
1835,	30 00 "
1841,	41 00 "
1845,	38 00 "
1846,	40 00 "
1848,	41 50 "
1850,	41 00 "

Prices remained at the quotation of 1850 with tendencies to $42, until, by the events of the war, they reached $64 per ton.

A communication from the town clerk of Essex, informs me that the ten-hour system was finally adopted in that place in the year 1847. It will be seen that the general tendency upward in prices received no impulse comparing with the reduction in hours—the advance between 1830 and 1841 being more than the advance from 1845 to 1850.

The California excitement began in 1848, occasioning a demand for vessels and a scarcity of workmen, and had, without doubt, more to do with the temporary rise of a dollar and a half a ton than the ten-hour change.

These figures are too limited to furnish anything more than an outline of the results desired; but fortunately, the benefits of the movement are too obvious to call for elaborate proof.

The remarks of D'Israeli in the English parliament, after three years experience of the working of the factory bill, will be recognized as applicable to us. "This Act having, as it is admitted, most successfully proved by experience that its consequences have been concomitant with the greatest commercial prosperity, with not only the maintenance, but the increase of exported commodities to those markets where, we have been told, the demand for them would be most materially injured by the adoption of the law, without any complaint against the action of this law, by a strange combination of circumstances, we are now called on to give a verdict on its character." (Hansard's Debates, p. 1,280, vol. 4, 1850.)

It is worthy of further remark in this connection, that the passage of the English Factory Bill happened soon after the repeal of the Corn Laws, which cheapened food, and, so far as this went, tended to lower wages by enabling the operatives to live for less; but the results were the contrary. Earl Shaftsbury says: "Is it not a fact, that wages so far from being reduced, where the hours of labor have been reduced, are greatly increased upon what they were before the period of limitation."

The dense populations of England have stimulated by their misery the inquiries of the statesmen of that country. Their permanancy of residence, compared with our own people, gives value to statistics; and these, in their turn, have given birth to social truths of great importance. In a debate in 1847, in the British House of Lords, on the ten-hour factory bill, Earl Ellesmere announced a principle, which further experience has amply confirmed:—

"*It is a remarkable fact, everywhere, and at all times the same, the more hours men work in any staple branch of manufactures, the less they receive in the form of wages.*"

An influential association has been formed in England, to stay the tide of Sabbath demoralization ; it has grappled for years, in the most practical and energetic manner, with the points of inquiry suggested by its objects. Appealing to the British workingmen, its motto is, that in cases of Sabbath labor, seven days' work is done for six days' pay. Its secretary, Mr. Charles Hill, 13 Bedford Row, London, writes to the Commission :—

"The statement of Earl Ellesmere, is one of the soundest principles of political economy."

It may be that ignorance and unfaithfulness are among the causes of the duration and scantiness of reward, of a large portion of our labor. These conditions have been deemed sufficient to account for its situation. The clearer light of the present day, warrants the conclusion, that this is but partially true. The letter of Mr. Hill remarks, that,—

" Railway servants, bakers, shop assistants, and others, who work on Sundays, and also excessive hours during the week, are very badly paid."

These classes of employ are sufficiently elevated in the social scale, to include skilled workmen, persons of easy manners, as salesmen, &c. ; and those in positions of pecuniary responsibility, as conductors, and others. They have, of course, their full share of the intelligence and character of the community ; yet they are depressed in wages and circumstances. The condition of the bakers, both in England and this country, is too notorious too need details. An English short-time tract, says :—

" The railway porter must be at his post before the train starts, and wait its arrival, however late it may be. Imagine a man with a wife and family to support, earning sixteen to eighteen shillings per week, having to be at work at six o'clock in the morning, and leaving off at twelve at night, working Sunday and week days."

I learn from another source, that the farm laborers of England are going into the manufacturing districts, where the hours of labor are ten, and earning from twenty to twenty-five shillings per week. Our own horse-car conductors and drivers, working fourteen hours, have but one dollar and seventy-five cents per day, while the ten-hour workmen in the vicinity, are receiving from $2.50 to $3.50 per day.

I find tailors at work in this city, at $2.00 for ten hours, a rate of wages much below the price of other descriptions of skilled labor, and evidently due to the fact that ten hours is only nominally adhered to; the extra work, to the extent of fifteen or more hours, which is going on, operating as an industrial maelstrom, to engulf its victims, by its consequences of lowering wages and (as was very evident,) health, and character also.

I have before me English documents, showing that at least four hours on Saturday afternoon, has been extensively deducted without lowering the wages. Mr. Lilwall, acting as spokesman for a deputation of noblemen and gentlemen, assured the English Secretary of State, Sir George Grey, in response to the question, whether, in case of a half-holiday being granted to workmen and others on Saturday, it was expected that they would receive the same remuneration as though they worked six full days, replied, that he believed that in all cases where the half-holiday had been granted, no reduction had been made in the pay.

The following from the "London Bee Hive," of June, 1866, is in the same direction, though not explicitly stated:—

"At Glasgow, on Friday last, the stone-cutters' six months' notice expired, by which they made the request of working nine hours per day, and the half-holiday on Saturday. A deputatien of the men waited on the various employers, and with one exception, it was agreed to accede to the request. At Edinburg, the masons have had the nine hours for some time past, as well as the half-holiday. They are a particularly well informed body of men, having their own hall for meetings, and a mutual improvement, and co-operative building society. I have been at some pains to inquire where nine hours is the practice, and find that the masons, both in Scotland and the north of England, are far in advance of all other trades. The following is an incomplete list of towns where they are working under the nine hour system. Rochdale, Bradford, Oldham, Huddersfield, Devesbury, Bolton, Halifax, Heywood, Accrington, Burnley, Aston, Wigan, Preston, Staleybridge, Mosely, Blackpool, Bury, and many more places in and about Lancashire and Yorkshire, while the Saturday half-holiday is universal."

It may with some propriety be said, that parallels should be drawn between those in the same shop or the same description of labor. It is difficult to do this, because, as circumstances approximate, as they necessarily do in business, time and wages settle themselves upon a common foundation. I have admitted that, a man considered in his individual capacity can do more in a single day of twelve hours than in one of ten. If he is at work by the piece, and in some cases by the day, he will of course earn and receive the most in the longest day. We have seen that this is not the case with laborers as a whole. What is the reason? I conclude that the conditions of continuous associated labor change so much, that calculations which are for a limited time true of the individual, in the end reverse themselves.

A manufacturer may have fifty females in his employ engaged on piecework. His prices may be such, that all of fair ability can earn eight dollars a week without excessive application. Ten of these employees, for various reasons, may be so desirous of an increased income as to be willing to overwork; if the duration of labor is fixed, they fill every moment of it; are always prompt in the morning; work perhaps a part of the noon hour, and labor through the day with an undue intensity of will and application. Saturday night their earnings are found to be ten dollars. There is a fair presumption that, after leaving out perhaps another ten, not up to the average strength or efficiency, the remaining thirty have accomplished as much as they could and preserve their health.

But will this make the slightest difference in the view which will be taken of the situation by a large class of employers? As these cases are apt to be decided, the ten laborious ones will fill their horizon,—" eight dollars is reckoned liberal pay; many of my neighbors only give prices amounting to five or six dollars per week; why should I reduce my profits by extra liberality?"

The usual result is to lower his prices, so that those who are drawing upon their future vitality can only earn their former weekly wages of eight dollars, and the reduction pro rata throughout the shop depresses to the lowest limit one-half of the employ.

Any one who has observed similar transactions to this in large shops, will have no difficulty in conceiving how, when the barrier of fixed hours is removed,—as in the cases of the London bakers and sewing women,—in England and in our own country, the longer the hours that are worked, the less the pay. There seems to be a vibratory action, from long hours to reduced pay, and from reduced pay to long hours again, as disastrous as the regular step of soldiery has sometimes proved on a treacherous bridge.

I wish to note here, what I could not with equal propriety do in the allusion to the advantages of ten hours, in the article on the hours of farm labor. So far as a standard of labor has been established, either by executive authority, by legislation for minors, or by the good sense of adults in connection with such rules, it has proved a barrier to the evils of overtime and consequent reduction of wages. The working classes, without a standard of time for a day's labor, are at the mercy of the employing interest.

There is an indefiniteness attaching to a day's work, when it varies with every day in the year,—as was the case when its duration was from sun to sun,—which is fatal to the independence of the laborer. The masses are morally in a minority, though not numerically so, and they need all the aid from rules properly adhered to, which the weakest party in a legislative body finds essential to its integrity.

Returning to the question of the relation of the hours of labor to wages, I infer, that the idea which is held by many liberal men outside the ranks of labor, that this dispute could be settled by making a unit of the hour, and allowing all to work as long as they please, is erroneous.

Aside from its impracticability for minor reasons, it has been shown to be at variance with our highest principles, and to stimulate some of our most pernicious infirmities. If the conditions of society really admitted the payment to the mass of laborers in this State for the next five years, of twelve or fourteen-tenths of the present wages for a corresponding increase of their hours of labor, there can be but little doubt, that instead of seeing our mills reducing to ten, and the cities agitating for eight, the reverse would be the case. So inflexible are the conditions which control the wages of labor, that it has been found useless to increase the poor rates in England,—as wages although at the starvation point before immediately lowered, as much as they were increased, by the additional rate.

I am aware that these views of the lowering tendencies of a merely competitive system, will be contested by all those who believe that wages are excessive, that labor, in this country, has its own way, &c.

To such, it must be said, that there is nothing in the avowed principles of society at the present time to justify their ideas. Every one knows what is meant by the unremunerative callings. It is universally understood that the laborer has only a living. The idea of what a living is, is comparatively elevated in this country; but figures show that the wages of labor do not reach on the whole that point. It will be admitted, that they sometimes are as high as can be expected under present circumstances; but these cases are always exceptional, and succeeded by periods of depression.

A further admission may be made in favor of those trades which have a natural tariff in the ability required for their exercise, as musical instrument makers, &c. Beyond these classes, the circumstances which enable any to accumulate after marriage are exceptional.

A considerable portion of the most respectable element of labor is sustained by family or social influences in steadiness of employ, and a rate of wages, or perquisites and privileges, materially relieving its situation.

The lower element of labor, in its very abjectness, the narrow field of its wants and its relation to wages, graded to a higher style of life, finds, in many cases, room for saving, increased by the wretched expedients inbred by ages of depression.

The appeal in this debate is to the average wages indicated in industrial returns, or reliable individual statements, and, in such inquiries, as might give us the character of the savings bank deposits.

When sixty-five million of dollars are without any minutiæ of statement credited to laborers, it seems no more than reasonable, in view of the fact that the savings banks are open to all classes, that some means should be provided by which the calling of the depositors, and the amount and character of the individual deposits, should be known.

Dr. William Elder, of Philadelphia, recently of the Treasury Department, at Washington, has kindly furnished me with the following statement, and the accompanying figures, relating to manufactures of cotton, woollen, clothing, shoes, &c., throughout the United States. Finding the total cost of labor, for the census year 1860, put at $378,878,966; the whole number of males at 1,040,349; the whole number of females 270,897; and finding the proportion of male, and female wages, in the compendium of the census of 1850, I assume not the rate, but the relative rate to remain the same in 1860, which was for females $\frac{5}{9}$ of that for males. By this rule, I deduce the average wages of the sexes in all employments.

Thus treated, the average wages of males throughout the United States, in these descriptions of labor, in 1860, were per annum, ... $316 15
Females, ... 176 75
Males per week, $6.12, per diem, ... 1 02
Females, " . 3.40, " 57

The wages for Massachusetts, for other than factory work, are thus given:—

Carpenters without board, . . . $1 70 per diem.
Monthly farm labor, with board, . . . 15 34 "
Day labor, with board, ... 90 "
Day labor, without board, ... 1 18 "
Weekly wages of female domestics, with board, 1 58 "
Price of board to laboring men, per week, . 2 50 "

These figures are averages for the whole State, and on the calculations, the year has six times fifty-two, or 312 days.

The wages of the cotton mills, of the six New England States, deduced by the method stated from the census of 1860, give:

Total wages, $16,720,920; number of males, 29,886; number of females, 51,517; this would give male wages per annum, ... $285 75
Female, . . . · 158 75

This is a considerable departure from the average for the whole country, in all employments, but perhaps not too much.

Male wages per diem, ... 91¼ cents.
Female, " . . . . . . 51 "

The Thorndike Company, cotton mill, Thorndike, Massachusetts, make a return to the Commissioners of $3,631.98, paid to 150 persons, for a month's labor, on September, 1866. This is an average of $24.21, for men, women, and children, or $290.-52 per annum. The agent states that this account requires some allowance, as the average, is based on the assumption, that all the hands in the mill on the last day, were employed through the month.

A carding-room in the James' Steam Mill, Newburyport, furnishes the following figures: Two hands, $12.00 per week, two, $9.00, seventeen, $6.00, five, $4.00, seventeen, $2.25; the last are children. These figures are given as a medium between the spinning and weaving rooms. A female operative in a cotton mill at Holyoke, stated, that she was a soldier's widow, with two children; she tended four looms, and earned $9.00, because accustomed to the work; rent $4.00 a month; could not support herself by her pay alone, but partly by her State aid, and the kindness of friends, kept her children at school. It should be stated that it is possible for a few of the most energetic to tend six looms, with corresponding wages.

The pay roll at the Charlestown Navy Yard, for October, 1866, amounted to $132,972, the earnings of 2,046 men; this is an average of a trifle more than $65.00 per month, $15.60 per week, or $780.00 per year. This average is computed on those who were on the pay roll, at the beginning of the month.

Tenements in the suburbs range in yearly rent, from $150.00 to $200.00; rather over than under, as it is very difficult to get a house large enough, for a family of six or eight, for less than $250.00.

The following items furnished by a housekeeper, are considered an underestimate, for a family of the number named:—

1½ bags of flour, per week, ... $3 00
1 pound of meat per day, at 25 cents, ... 1 75
½ bushel of potatoes, ... 50
2 pounds butter, ... 1 00
2 " sugar, ... 36

¼ pound of tea, ... $0 30
1 quart of milk per day, at 8 cents, ... 56
                                              ─────
                                              $7 47
   Estimating weekly rent, at 4 00

The amount per week, for the two items of rent, and living, will be $11.47, leaving a balance of $4.13 per week, for the items of expense or loss, connected with public worship, clothing, fuel, tools, travelling, — daily and otherwise — newspapers, school-books, sickness, hired help in the family, time out of employ, holidays, &c. Deducting less than a third of the number, who are earning about $900.00 per year, and passing over an intermediate portion, we should find nearly one-half receiving less than $50.00 per month.

The wages of a first-class ship-carpenter, working under very favorable circumstances as to health, acquaintance, &c., in Boston and vicinity, on repairs, at three dollars per day, at a time when wages were $2.25 at new work, are stated in the following extract from a letter to the Commission :—

"The earnings of the writer, receiving the highest wages paid to any out-door journeyman mechanic, for several years subsequent to 1850, averaged eight hundred dollars per year, decreasing from 1856 to 1860, when it was but $485.

"With a family of eight, entirely dependent upon these earnings for support, with the exception of house rent. Of this, $30 was paid for city tax, $36 for pew tax, $12 for benevolent and Christian objects, $10 for school books, $10 for papers and periodicals, and something for charitable objects and for tools, reducing the amount to be appropiated to the actual necessaries of life, by more than a hundred dollars, and leaving less than fifty dollars to each person to procure comfortable food and clothing, necessary to maintain a respectable standing in society. This has necessitated a system of economy, which has left painful evidence of its severity; and with constant employment, the condition of things has been growing worse since 1860; has compelled the removal of children from school, and made it necessary for all who could to contribute to their support."

The following schedule of wages, is from a workman in a trade connected with ship-building; and gives the yearly wages of a first-class mechanic at day's work :—

In the year 1852, daily wages $2.00, . . . $450 00
　　　　　1853,　　　"　　　2.25,　. . . 525 00
　　　　　1854,　　　"　　　3.00,　. . . 700 00
　　　　　1855,　　　"　　　2.00,　. . . 450 00
　　　　　1856,　　　"　　　2.00,　. . . 450 00
　　　　　1857,　　　"　　　1.75,　. . . 450 00
　　　　　1858,　　　"　　　1.75,　. . . 450 00
　　　　　1859,　　　"　　　1.50,　. . . 425 00
　　　　　1860,　　　"　　　1.50,　. . . 375 00
　　　　　1861,　　　"　　　2.25,　. . . 500 00

These figures, although given in round numbers, are drawn from accounts, not now accessible, and are known to approximate very nearly the facts.

The items of expense were as follows:—
House rent, $75.00; pew tax, benevolent purposes, &c., $30.00; coal (2½ tons yearly) and wood, $25.00; clothing for two, $60.00; literature, newspapers, &c., $12.00.

Calculating the yearly income at $450.00, these items will leave a surplus of about $250.00, which allows 68cts. a day for the food of two persons, and incidentals, such as tools, travelling, sickness, &c. The experience of this couple for these ten years, as detailed to me, shows that it was impossible for a married pair to live with common decency in our large towns at that time, for less than $1.25 for every day's expenses, Sundays included; and that with constant thoughtfulness, this income necessitated an economy penurious in its character, often failing to meet the demands of health, in clothing; and throwing the support of aged parents on to more favored relations. This pressure was so great as to demand the income of the prosperous years, up to $525.00, leaving no savings, except during the year 1854.

It would be incorrect to assume that the highest figures of the Navy Yard estimate can be applied to an equal number of workmen in civil employ; work is sought there, in preference to all other places, because of its permanency. The number of workmen who have an income of $900.00 now, or who received $600.00 formerly, forms probably less than an eighth of the whole number in the community; and the pecuniary prosperity of these, is due to the exceptional causes I have named, to overtime, or to excessive labor at piece or job work.

These conditions are regarded by the industrial interest as proving that no remedy for our national or private burdens can be found in stimulated immigration. Labor is already poorly paid; further to depress wages, would involve all in loss.

Wages, as at present paid, are not what they are claimed to be,—an equitable return for labor performed; but they are, in the main, the result of forces of the nature of an inexorable necessity. It seems impossible permanently to depress or elevate them beyond a point, which may be taken as an average of all the influences coming from the character of the working classes, and the immediate connections of a commercial nature affecting business. It seems conclusive, that their amount, arguing comprehensively, is not increased by lengthening the hours, but lessened; and it is also seen, that temporary causes may, and often do, raise and lower wages very perceptibly, while any reduction in hours which has yet taken place, has tended decidedly to raise them by aids coming from the wider circle of wants, and the increased productiveness of labor thus enhanced in its average intelligence and efficiency.

It is evident, that the decision of the length of time which shall be held to constitute a day's work, is not simply a commercial question. Viewed by this light alone, the condition of the masses is hopeless, because pure commerce is pure selfishness. The interest which attaches to the signatures of Queen Victoria to the Factory Bill, and President Van Buren to the Order for the Public Works, arises from the relation which those measures bore to the liberation of great populations of adults from the absolute control of pecuniary influences; thus making the length of a day's labor a "brain question," to be decided in the interests of intelligence and morals, and tending by its influence to restrain within reasonable limits, the natural rise and fall of wages, in obedience to commercial laws.

A Legal Standard.

The industrial interests ask for the enactment of a Legal Standard, defining under certain circumstances the duration of a day's labor. They do this because they find that in making their own contracts, they, as individuals and as a class, are powerless to effect the change of time desired.

If the number of hours constituting a day's work was a matter concerning themselves alone, they might not press this request; many instances have occurred where parties were willing to make the sacrifice of wages implied in the recognition of the reduction as a purely business matter, but were denied the privilege.

This is the case with most of the operatives in the mills; large classes of employ in the cities are also in the same situation, even when working by the piece.

In consequence of this, there is a decided conviction that it is hopeless to contend against opposing influences unaided by the authority and example of the municipal, State, and national governments. In England, agitation was carried on for nearly half a century, resulting in such control of the hours of labor by legislation for minors as finally to establish in 1847 ten hours in the factory districts as the customary limit of a day's labor. In this country, fourteen years of vigorous agitation by a large number of the most influential trades failed to accomplish the change. The political crisis of 1840, opportune in this respect, prompted the order limiting the hours of labor in the national works to ten. Public opinion at that time but very partially supported this action, and the view is held by those best qualified to judge, that the cause was otherwise hopeless at the moment when ultimate success was assured by this humane regulation.

Causes, local and exceptional in their character, have induced to a slight extent in a few limited trades, further reductions to nine and eight hours. These successes have been mostly in England, and are due to the extraordinary vigor of the trade unions, which have absorbed the force which in this country is exercised by the ballot. The pressure at the present time for legislation affords sufficient proof of the prevalence of the opinion formed under such precedents;' that the reform can only be effected in connection with the discussion and ultimate action, which its commanding relation to national prosperity implies and necessitates.

The first national labor congress, composed of delegates from all parts of the Union, which convened at Baltimore in August,

1866, announced the following as a portion of the first of a list of thirteen resolutions:—

"Our object is to scure the enactment of laws by our national congress, and several State legislatures, making eight hours a legal day's work."

This, with the other resolutions, after deliberation, was passed with but one dissenting vote. Those who petition for the enactment of a standard of labor, argue that it is unjust and unwise to leave time, in its relation to human effort, without at least some kind of legal recognition such as has been granted to space, measure, weight, interest and coin. By confining legislation to these points, a great preponderance of benefit has resulted to those possessing wealth. Not necessarily, however, to them alone. By common consent laws have been enacted defining what shall constitute a barrel, a bushel, etc. With less unanimity, rates of interest have been established, and maintained with sufficient accuracy to illustrate the principle. The same motives have resulted in the legal control of coin by its weight and purity. Why is it that up to the present moment, instead of relaxing the theory, and practice in reference to a bushel as a measure, it has been still further conserved by the enactment of the number of pounds which shall be deemed to constitute a bushel? Dealers say, the measure has been brought into nearer relationship to the pound because errors and frauds are thereby lessened. In saying this, they practically indorse the following statement:—

"The government appoints inspectors to see that the quality of the articles sold, and the capacity of the standards in use, are kept up to an established point. Why is it necessary to do this? Because the greed of gain knows no bounds; it is insatiable, and grows with what it feeds upon. It would reduce a barrel of flour to half its present size, and adulterate it at that. It would reduce weights and measures to such dimensions that we should have the homœopathic principle of infinitesimal doses in everything."

It is not necessary to suppose a general laxity of morals among traders to bring about a state of things approximating to the above. Upright men, even though in a majority, need all the force of supervisory laws to aid them in resisting the current of avarice.

If the influential interests of trade thus depend upon legislation to remove the abuses caused by selfishness, may not labor present its own case as parallel? Is it any discredit to its intelligence or self-respect that its voice is heard pressing the request for such laws as will place it on a level with the other interests so carefully guarded by legislation?

Can it be assumed with truthfulness, that the working men and women in this country are properly secured in the possession of their rights in this respect, when the following remarks can be made concerning a large class of them by a dispassionate observer, even in our own favored State:—

"We cannot safely neglect the interests of field hands; no class has suffered more wrong in the past; the bitterest, most obdurate forms of slavery have frequently fallen to their lot. Engaged in rough, hard labor, which admits of coarse and careless execution, separated from each other and made incapable of combination, removed from the observation of men, and that general intercourse which quickens and develops the mind, these laborers have been, even to our own time and country, *especially unable to protect themselves* and secure the full advantage of their toil."

That it is so assumed, can be shown by the testimony of Mr. Wetherell, in the reports of the first commission, folio 5, page 19: "Therefore leave that alone which is well as it is; let the laborer make a contract if he wishes for five, six, ten hours, just as he pleases: leave him free to do according to his own will."

The same gentleman reveals how large a share the "laborer's wishes" have in the conclusion of a bargain in another place in the same reports, by admitting that the ten-hour system, as introduced into Massachusetts and elsewhere, has not affected the number of hours worked on the farm in the slightest. After a partial admission relating to the war, he goes on stating, that he has no authority to say that they—the farmers—have any idea of a day's work being less than that which comes between sun and sun.

A lecture was delivered in London in 1848 by Dr. William A. Guy, at a meeting presided over by Lord Ashley. As a physician in one of the public hospitals of that city, Dr. Guy became interested in the situation of the journeymen bakers, and made it a matter of personal investigation for facts, and of inquiry as to principles bearing on their condition. His lecture, a pamphlet of thirty-one pages, was reprinted in 1860, without alteration. He says, in a prefatory note, " that he sees no reason to correct the statements or to modify the opinions expressed twelve years before. Both have been confirmed by further inquiry, experience and reflection, and he is still of opinion that the proper remedy for the evils complained of is is to be found in legislation." His views will be seen to support the principle that labor is urging :—

"I put it to you, my friends, whether you can make your own bargains with your employers in any reasonable or practical sense of the term? I will take a case. I will suppose that I am a master baker, and that any one of you is a journeyman out of work. I have a place to dispose of, and you are anxious to engage yourself. I am satisfied that your character is good, and that you understand your business. I agree to take you on the usual terms. You are quite willing to close with me, but you say that you cannot, in justice to your health, which you are bound to preserve, work eighteen or twenty hours out of the twenty-four. What answer should I be compelled to give? Should I not decline to employ you, except according to the usages of the trade? To be sure I should; and I should probably tell you of a neighbor, who, as it is, was running me very hard by working men more, on an average, than eighteen or twenty hours a day, and whom I could no more compel to change his system than you could compel me to take you into my employ. The bad habits and usages of the trade are too strong for both of us. I say, then, it is bitter mockery to talk about grown-up men being able to make their own bargains. The premises are false, and the conclusion falls to the ground.

" But perhaps I shall be met by the argument, that, though the individual is powerless, the body of workmen or employers is not. They can arrange the matter among themselves. It seems to me to argue great ignorance of human nature to suppose this probable or even possible. Who does not know the bigoted opposition of which a minority of a few score of ignorant, selfish and self-willed men is capable? It may be still objected, that if the masters and journeymen cannot be brought to agree, the journeymen may take the matter into their own hands, and strike. But is not this the very last thing the truly practical man would encourage. I contend, then, that without legislative interference, your case is hopeless. The individual journeyman cannot, as is absurdly contended by your opponents, make his own bargains. The whole body of journeymen cannot win over the whole body of masters to the side of humanity and justice; and strikes have failed, and will failed again, and are at best but temporary remedies."

Co-operation has been suggested as a feasible means of grafting the innovation upon the habits of society: but most of those who propose it little realize the obstacles. It is simply to say to a man who desires to raise a weight, which he knows he cannot, double it, and you will accomplish your wish. Aids to co-operation are seen to follow reductions of hours; but as yet they have advanced no farther in practical results in manufactures than to render the informal union of small parties of job workmen practicable, the brevity of the undertakings and the fact that fixed capital is not required, entering largely into the causes of their success.

The thoughtfulness and intelligent self-control necessary to guide energy to successful business results has not yet been attained by any considerable portion of the industrial community. The business interests are certainly far in advance of them in these respects; but the system of agencies and of proxy voting, by which our corporations are carried on, indicate despotic rather than co-operative developments. Realizing these facts, judicious workmen do not feel it prudent to expose an idea, which they regard as initiative in its nature, to a double hazard of postponement by the defeats which it is foreseen will result in the first efforts at co-operation in manufactures.

We now come to a consideration of the character and results of the legislation desired. What good will it do simply to enact that eight hours (in the absence of contracts,) shall constitute a day's work? It is claimed that the simple announcement of the fact that Massachusetts recognized eight hours as a suitable average for certain kinds of labor, would exert a great influence in forming and guiding opinion to beneficial results.

The development of the public mind, in all the industrial civilizations of Europe and America, is turning as on a pivot on those facts and principles which centre on reductions of hours. To name one of them in this country,—the unequal distribution of wealth, with its demoralizing results, so fearfully contrasting with our political and religious privileges.

The expression of unanimous opinion, on the part of a joint committee of the legislature of 1865, in this direction, has appealed in multiplied copies to humanity throughout all these regions, and has everywhere awakened a sympathetic response, not alone from the masses, but from many of the gifted and refined.

The authoritative promulgation of correct theories, is thus seen to develop one of the ruling forces of the world. But it would not stop here. If the inertia of society should prevent the State from regulating her dealings with the individual, by her own standard, her inconsistency would be the subject of comment, and she could not long refrain from compliance with her own rules; thus adding the force of example, to sustain the wisdom of her declaratory enactment.

That the application of these views to practice, is not fanciful, but commands the assent and active support of the statesmen and business men, of the most intensely practical people in the world, may be seen by the following account of a Deputation to Sir George Grey:—

"Yesterday, a deputation from the Early Closing Association, waited upon the Secretary of State for the Home Department, at his official residence. The deputation consisted of the Earl of Shaftsbury; the Marquis of Blandford, M. P.; the Hon. Arthur Kinnaird, M. P.; Capt. Stuart, M. P.; Sir Andrew Agnew, Bart., M. P.; Rev. J. H. Gurney; Rev. T. Binney; Arthur Mills, Esq.; Robert Hanbury, Jun., Esq.; G. H. Davis, Esq.; B. Shaw, Esq.; Mr. J. R. Taylor; J. J. Mechi, Esq.; John Corderoy, Esq.; Wm. Locke, Esq.; Mr. Lilwall, Honorary Secretary, &c., &c.

"The Earl of Shaftsbury, who introduced the deputation, said that Sir George Grey must be aware of the efforts making in various quarters, to secure a half-holiday for the laboring classes of the community. The necessity of such relaxation from the pressure of business in these days of competition and energetic action, his lordship regarded as incontestible. The moral, social, civil and political welfare of the public, were all bound up in it. Mr. Mechi, his lordship observed, was present, and could testify from the experience of his own establishment, that such a half-holiday was practicable, and likely to be serviceable to employers. His lordship further observed, that it was not designed to ask for (coercive) legislative action, which, indeed, the nature of the case did not admit of, but if the government would use its influence, and, *above all, set the example*, by introducing the half-holiday into their offices; into the arsenals, dockyards, and all institutions under government control; the happiest results must follow.

"The Hon. Arthur Kinnaird concurred in all that fell from Earl Shaftsbury, and observed that the Saturday half-holiday had already been adopted in Glasgow, Dundee, and other Scotch towns, producing the greatest possible satisfaction to all parties; adding, that two o'clock was the hour at which it was proposed business should be suspended.

"Sir George Grey said, that with reference to the public offices with which he was more particularly connected, he thought it would not be practicable, especially during the sitting of Parliament, to close such offices at two o'clock on Saturday, besides which, he felt that the clerks employed in those offices were not much in need of a weekly half-holiday; and with regard to the other establishments connected with the state, such as the dockyards, it frequently happened that it was unavoidable, that the men therein employed had to work at all hours. These departments, however, were not under his control.

"Lord Shaftsbury replied, that respecting these establishments, application would be made in the proper quarter. Mr. Lilwall read a letter from Sir Samuel Morton Peto, Bart., of which the following is a copy:—

12, KENSINGTON PALACE GARDENS, 20th MAY, 1856.

MY DEAR SIR:—I greatly regret that I have an important appointment, at the time you meet Sir George Grey, and that the shortness of your notice prevents my attempting any re-arrangement of my engagements. I feel deeply, the importance of the Saturday half-holiday. It is not a subject for legislation; *but if the government will set the example in all their establishments, the greatest good will result.*

On all our works we have shortened the Saturday work to four in the afternoon, and in our offices to one o'clock. I do not see any difficulty in adopting the half-holiday; it only requires a little arranging of the time during the week to do it. I know the workmen, as a body, will use it well, *and we are bound to supplement our exertions in the cause of education, by giving this boon, at least.* I wish you success. I know Sir George is earnestly desirous of elevating the industrial classes.   I am, dear sir, truly yours,   S. MORTON PETO.
JOHN LILWALL, ESQ.

"The Rev. J. Hampden Gurney observed, that although it doubtless was true that in certain public offices the hours were already such that they could not be complained of, yet he thought it would be found, if Sir George directed his attention to the subject, that there were other departments connected with the government where a half-holiday on Saturdays would be a great boon. Mr. Mechi remarked, that the amount of work done did not altogether depend upon the period devoted to it, but was greatly regulated by the extent of energy and attention that were brought to bear upon it. He added, that the advancement which had taken place in science during the last few years, would fall short of the benefit it was calculated to confer, if it did not lead to an abridgement of the period of human labor.

"Sir George Grey inquired, whether, in case of a half-holiday being granted to workmen, and others, on Saturday, it was expected that they would receive the same remuneration as though they worked six full days?

Mr. Lilwall replied, that he believed that in all cases, where the half-holiday had been granted, no reduction had been made in the pay, for the reason *that it was found that the men exerting themselves with greater energy, really did as much work, as before they did in six.* Mr. Lilwall said, the latter view was borne out by the recorded testimony of a large number of firms of eminence, who had either wholly, or in part, adopted the half-holiday. He thought that in the case of the dockyards, the very circumstance that the exigencies of the service rendered it imperative that the men should work on Sundays, was itself a strong reason why the half-holiday should be given, when such pressure did not exist.

G. H. Davis, Esq., said that when the half-holiday was first mooted in the establishment with which he was connected, fears were entertained that it might interfere with the dispatch of business, but those fears were not realized; and that it was found that three or four persons taking the necessary duties in turns, enabled the institution to set at liberty between forty and fifty persons, who were thus able to enjoy their Saturday afternoon. The object of the deputation was not to secure a half-holiday for gentlemen whose hours were from ten to four, or who are only occasionally required to remain late; but to obtain the influence of government example. The importance of the movement to the welfare of society, he thought, had been well stated by the Earl of Shaftsbury, and justified the government in taking it into their serious consideration.

"The deputation, then withdrew."

There is little or no difference of opinion, as to the right of the State, to control the hours of minors. There are a considerable number of these, estimated on page xc., of the Report of the Board of State Charities, at fifteen hundred new comers each year, to be provided for. That there is occasion for the exercise of such supervision, may be seen from the following extract, from the same report:—

"It sometimes happens that the leading motive for men to take apprentices, under the present system, is that of gain. Men talk the matter over with their wives, and conclude that if they can have an active boy from the Reform School, or the State Almshouse, to do light work, run errands, and the like, his services will more than pay for his board and clothing. Setting out with these views, a sort of antagonism is generated. The family is afraid they shall not get enough out of the boy, and are apt to make him a drudge. They require him to work harder than any one else in the family, but have poorer fare. Without any intentional cruelty on their part, *he is liable to be overworked*, underfed, poorly clad, and stinted of his Sunday leisure, and his winter schooling. Unless the family are persons of more than ordinary delicacy and sensibility, the apprentice is liable to be reminded that he is only a Reform School boy, or a State Pauper, and to be dwarfed in his moral nature, for lack of sympathy and consideration. The drudge in the eyes of others is apt to be one in his own."—" These are indeed, exceptional cases, for, as a general rule, the apprentices do well, better than if kept under confinement, especially if they are so situated that they can easily make their condition and treatment known to responsible persons. They are subjected to the ordinary social and domestic influences of the class of persons to whom they are apprenticed, and must take their chance, for good and for evil, just as ordinary boys must do."

An emigrant landing on our shores, or a lad leaving our public schools, if inclined to trade, finds a system of legislation ready for their use. An English operative, under the same circumstances, who has enjoyed the advantages of legislation, discovers, to his surprise, that increase of political liberty means, in its every-day relations, a loss of some of his dearest privileges, in his abandonment to long hours and overtime. Private interest, in money-making, commands the intellectual forces of society, from the decision of the length of a yardstick to the complications of the bonded warehouse system. Mutual agreements between nations provide for commerce and literature, and against crime, while the less pretentious interests of labor scarcely excite a thought, nor receive any advantage, except as they are remotely connected with the general good, and this in many respects only by inversion, as it seems that some of the grandest triumphs of science and art are so completely at the disposal of gain, that they can only be relied on to aid in human progress by intensifying evil to such an extent as to arouse opposition, and thus give birth to reform.

The frequent use of terms implying mutuality of connection in significant circumstances during the public humiliations and

dangers of the war, indicate a deeper obligation of society, as embodied in government, than has yet been complied with; and on no question has this indifference been more noticeable than on the one under consideration. The able sanitary survey of the State, of the year 1850, a volume of five hundred and forty pages, has no allusion to the subject that I can find, beyond a single paragraph giving the time-table of the Lawrence Mills, without comment.

The recent circular of Mr. Beckwith, the American agent at the Paris Exposition, includes twenty-one points of inquiry but omits the hours of labor.

The Memorial of the Boston Sanitary Association, (House 112, 1861,) is similarly defective, but nobly redeems itself by an annunciation and defence of principles of the greatest importance. Three brief extracts will suffice :—

"They respectfully represent that the interests of human health and life, and the vital statistics and condition of the people of this Commonwealth, in their opinion, require more of the paternal care, watchfulness and protection of the legislature than they now receive."

"Trade, commerce, agriculture, manufactures and other means and methods of creating money, in every shape, have been and are watched, encouraged and aided by whatever legislation they seem to need, while the health and power, the comfort and availability of the man himself, by whom and for whom all this is done, is made a matter of secondary consideration, in a national point of view."

"Our civilization hitherto has not felt a due responsibility for these destructive influences, which, in manifold ways of sorrow and pain, weigh heavily on every class of society; but, in another step of advancement, it will look after and grapple with them, and apply its resources of intelligence and power to modify and diminish them. That work is yet to be done. These evils are still present with us. They endanger the people's safety; they mar their happiness; they very seriously curtail the blessings of life, which the constitution specifies as among the objects of the institution and maintenance of government."

Guided by the erroneous or partial views thus impressively alluded to, State authority has given existence to institutions so absolute in their control of industry as to give rise to just apprehensions for the consequences, and to necessitate counterbalancing legislation. These fears seem reasonable in the light of the misapprehensions pervading society. Because the restrictions of the Old World pauper system are not felt here, and a laborer may travel without inquisition, or locate without ejectment; it is forgotten that the power exists, and is sometimes exercised, in all our large manufacturing cities, to close the gates of every mill in the place at the briefest notice, or at no notice at all, to any operative, without any of the provision for the weak, as against the strong, which would be gained by an impartial oversight of labor, with proper publicity, while combined operations in coal and grain and gold throw off even the semblence of secrecy. The misapprehensions alluded to find expression in the following sentences, denouncing organizations of labor:—

"We live in a more free and intelligent age, and under institutions which encourage and foster the largest personal freedom. Merchants and manufacturers have long since abandoned these oppressive and effete organizations; and the sooner their example is followed by mechanics, the sooner will these latter be in a position to advance their interests according to their merits."

Is Human Labor a Commodity?

Can it properly be bought and sold with as little regard to elevated considerations as merchandise? If it can, then invidious comment on the course of the millionaire, who has built up his fortune on the profits of the labor of sewing women, is uncalled for.

The fact that the millionaire's course is quite extensively the subject of criticism, and that in quarters not by any means radical, affords room for the opinion that society distrusts itself, however tenaciously it may defend the laws of supply and demand, as sufficient to control this question. Arguing from the prosperous side, it has been said that "the world is one vast co-operative association, so admirably adjusted that it is impossible for any party to take advantage of the other." The sewing women and sundry other interested parties deny this; nor is the denial confined to one class. Professor Fawcett, M. P., has recently said,—

"That he never heard the Chancellor of the Exchequer bring forward his budget, and show in terms most eloquent the vast increase of our national wealth, without the sad reflection that, whilst one class was growing immensely rich on the labor of the country, the accumulation of riches did not do so much as it ought to do to diminish the poverty of the land, and lessen the hours of toil."

It forms an interesting subject of inquiry, whether the ideas and sentiments which it is clear are busy on this problem have found any development in this State on the plane of the interests involved in this inquiry. Intellectual labor seems to be met in a higher spirit than is usually found in the market-place. We do not accept the lowest bidder to fill our pulpits or conduct our schools. In theory, certainly, and to some extent actually, we govern ourselves by motives of a personal and moral character. The question has been widely asked, what had school teachers ought to have? not what can we get them for. If a merchant makes a loss in business, he does not immediately run to his clerk and say, "I must cut down your salary;" neither does he import clerks by wholesale for the sake of placing salaries at the minimum.

An approach to more elevated dealing with manual labor, may be found in the course of some of our corporations, in beautifying by shrubbery their grounds, providing books, &c.; but beyond the moral benefits incidental to a well-ordered community, the labor of the State cannot be said to enjoy any of the advantages which it is supposed will ensue from practical recognition of the doctrine that *human labor is so connected with exalted mental and moral capacities, that it of right ought to have higher consideration than merchandise.* An exception to this conclusion may be found in the successful union of labor and capital, on elevated principles, in the cod and mackerel fisheries of the State. Maritime usage and laws, have exercised a conservative influence in restraining impulses, which in ordinary affairs would lead to disagreement and disaster, and the general prosperity and good feeling ensuing, contrast strangely with the results of the whale fishery, even in the same ports; the last, being conducted on the usual commercial principles offers a share so disproportionate as only to command the services of adventurers for its laborious and hazardous duties.

It has long been known that in some of our distinctively fishing towns, conditions existed, much more favorable to industrial prosperity than in localities devoted to commerce or manufactures. In many of the towns first named, the young men are retained in the place of their birth under circumstances favorable to marriage, the owning of a residence, and the support of a family. In some of these communities the response to the inquiry, " What proportion of your people own their houses ? " will be, " Two-thirds." It may be questioned whether so large a portion as one-quarter of the remaining industry of the State are so favorably situated. The secret of this is to be found in the following peculiarity of the business. " After the articles needed for the voyage are paid for and the fish sold, the profits are divided in the proportion of three-eighths to the owners, and five-eighths to the crew."

It is certainly an interesting fact that we should go back to the description of industry which laid, in colonial times, the foundation of our prosperity, for the practical adoption of an idea which seems likely to be regarded as the culmination of our industrial civilization. In the explanation of this doctrine, facts and principles are happily blended by Mr. Harrison, an English writer on this subject :—

"As it is this interference with what is called Free Trade which is the main charge against unionism, it is important to examine this question in detail. It is often asked, ' why cannot the fifty shillings' worth of puddling be bought in the same manner as the fifty shillings' worth of pig iron ? ' Well, one thing is, that the pig iron can wait until next week or next month. It is in no immediate hurry. But the fifty shillings' worth of puddling cannot wait even a few days. The ' human machine ' in question is liable to the fatal defect of dying. Nor is it in all the relations of life that ' each man is free to bargain for himself.' It is curious in how many sides of our existence this liberty is curtailed. If one wants £1,000 worth of horse, one can go to Tattersall's and buy it without question. But if one wants £1,000 worth of wife, there will be a good many questions asked, and a good many people to consult. The lady's relations even may wish to say something ; there may be all sorts of stipulations, to say nothing of settlements. A man cannot buy a place in a partnership exactly in open market. He cannot go to a physician, or a lawyer, or a priest, and haggle about the fee. In fact, wherever there are close or permanent human relations between one man and many, an understanding with all jointly is the regular course. Every partnership of labor, all co-operation to effect anything in common, involves this mutual agreement between all. It is because employers fail to see that manufacture is only the combined labor of many of which they are the managers, that they regard the whole concerns, stock, plant and 'hands' as raw material, to be bought and sold. The iron-master who buys pig iron is not entering into permanent relations with it, or even with its possessor. It cannot work with him obey him, trust him. The 'human machine,' however, is a very surprising engine. It has a multitude of wants, a variety of feelings, and is capable of numerous impulses which are commonly called human nature. An iron-master cannot buy in open market fifty shillings' worth of puddling, because he does not want fifty shillings' worth of puddling. It would be of no good to him if he had it. He wants a man who will work, not his fifty shillings' worth of puddling, but day by day, and year by year; who will work when he is not himself overlooking him; who will work intelligently, and not ruin his machinery and waste his stock; who will not cheat him, or rob him, or murder him; who will work as a chance hireling will not and cannot work; who will trust him to act fairly and feel pride in his work, and in the place. If he cannot get men like these he knows that he will be ruined and undersold by those who can. He knows that fifty shillings' worth of black slave would not help him, nor fifty shillings' worth of steam-engine. Do what he will, perfect machinery to a miracle, still the manufacturer must ultimately depend on the co-operation of human brains and hearts. No 'human machinery' will serve his end. Can a general in war buy fifty shillings' worth of devoted soldiers? Can he make his bargain with each man of his army separately? They are too precious to be picked up in a moment, and their efficiency lies in their union. If the iron-master had to go into the labor market as often as he has to go into the iron market, and haggle for every day's work as he does for every pig and bar, he would be a dead or ruined man in a year. He cannot buy puddling as he can buy pigs, because in one word men are not pig iron. Sentiment, this, perhaps; but a sentiment which cannot be conquered, and produces stern facts. For the fifty shillings' worth of puddling by long reflection has discovered that to the making of iron goes the enduring, willing, intelligent labor of many trained men; that it is work which is impossible without a permanent combination of will and thought, but the produce of which may be unfairly divided unless all act with a spirit of mutual defence and protection. They see their employers too often forgetting this, the underlying fact of all industry, and their answer is, Unionism. Sentimental! emotional economy! but a fact. When pigs and bars of iron exhibit a similar phenomenon, an iron-master will buy his fifty shillings' worth of puddling as freely as he buys his pigs or his bars,—but not till then."

These views derive force from the evident truths that labor cannot be transferred; that it is not a substance that can be separated and carried away. A thing may be bought and sold, because it is a thing; but a man with his labor, cannot be bought and sold, without recognizing slavery as a right. Those profound utterances, which light the progress of the race, do not say that labor is worthy of its price; but the laborer is worthy of his hire.

The burden and the curse of the present ideas are, that they enslave the spirit, by repressing, if not forbidding the exercise of all but the most common-place emotions in daily relations. Our development of civilization, is not distinctively at fault, on the score of generosity, but a more elevated sense of justice, in social relations, seems to be the impulse needed at the present time

The practical application of this doctrine may be seen in the items below, from English and American labor organs. The first one being from the same authority as the second:—

"It is well known that if each workman gave his mind to his work and put his good will into it, for the benefit of his employers, they could together, create a new amount of profit. Take one instance. It has been calculated that the working colliers at Whitwood and Methley, could, by simply taking the trouble to get the coal in large lumps, and reducing the proportions of slack, add to the colliery profits £1,500 a year. If they would further take a little extra care below ground in keeping the best coal separate from the inferior, they could add another £1,500 to the profits. In these two instances alone, men working—not with good will instead of bad will, but with good will instead of no will—could create £3,000 a year. Now, a man of original business sagacity, looking at these facts—which are true, less or more, in all trades—would say, 'I discover herein a new method of making money I see my men can, if they had a motive to do it, create for me £3,000 a year. If I gave them £1,500 of it, they would have that motive; they would be delighted; I should appear a great benefactor in their eyes. And I *should* be a benefactor, too; for I should put in their way, and place it within their power, to add £1,500 a year to their wages. We should be on good terms after this.' This is the theory of the partnerships of industry, cleared of all sentimentality and the confusion of ideas which surround new discoveries in economical science. It is simply a wholesome utilitarian principle applied to industry. These partnerships are based on a principle from which all new civilization has sprung; a principle of intelligent selfishness. Good feeling alone will not conduct a large commercial concern; there needs self-interest tempered by good sense; and this good sense now perceives that a thousand workmen will produce to a concern, far more profit, if they have an interest in what they are doing, and have a motive to avoid waste of material, loss of time, and to work with all their skilfulness." * * * *

"Partnership of Labor. Mr. G. J. Holyoke has published, with this title, the paper he read at the Sheffield meeting of the Social Science Congress. We have published extracts of Mr. Holyoke's Essay, and should like to make another quotation, in order to call further attention to what we regard as one of the most hopeful signs of the new era in industrial progress—the co-operative colleries in Yorkshire. After noticing the initiation of the co-operative partnership principle by the Messrs. Crossley of Halifax, Mr. Holyoke remarks:—

"The Messrs. Henry Briggs & Son, proprietors of the Whitwood and Methley Colleries, have had the distinction of carrying the principle of industrial partnership further, and of being the first employers to recognize labor as property entitled to profits. Taking the average profits their capital ought to produce (they fix upon ten per cent. as the amount that must be realized,) they have converted their business into a company, and admit, like the Messrs. Crossley, all their workmen who choose to invest their savings in shares. And if they do not, or cannot, it is provided in the prospectus, that all profits over ten per cent. shall be divided between the shareholders who have risked their capital in the business, and the workmen whose devotion and skill have produced the profit. This is the first time any employers have thus formally recognized the poor man's labor as property. This is a distinction not to be mentioned without gratitude, and of immense significance in the industrial progress of the future. I have visited the Whitwood Colliery, as I wished to see for myself the spot where this sacred change has begun. I was allowed to descend into the pits, as I wished to judge of the security for life for which these colleries are known. Being invited by the men to make a speech to them, I addressed them as 'the first English men whose labor employers had recognized as their property, and counselled them to err for the first time on the side of confidence; to listen to no suspicions; to abate no exertion, that this new compact of Capital with Industry might succeed for the sake of their brethren; to respect themselves; to entertain no uncomfortable or ungenerous criticism of their masters' motives; but, like men of sense in the middle class, to fix their attention on the *tendency* of the scheme to promote their own benefit, and give their employers honorable credit for a proposal, whose tendency is the workingman's advantage. Made in the face of the nation, applauded by the most eminent friends of labor, the compact could never go back if they were faithful to it; and the noblest experiment commenced in our time, would be dated from those pits in which they worked. It was now in their power not only to raise their wages, but to raise their order.' I can bear my testimony from examination, that the system of accounts devised by the Messrs. Briggs, for enabling the men to secure the profit that may accrue to them, is simple, accessible and satisfactory. The experiment bids fair to succeed, as more coal has been worked since it was commenced, than has been worked before in the same time."—*The Co-Operator (Eng.)*, Dec. 15, 1865.

"While upon the subject of Co-operation, it occurs to me that our present system of day wages might, with propriety, be so arranged as to be partially co-operative, and being made so, would prove mutually beneficial to both employer and employed. It would also tend to check a disposition to ramble, that is getting to be a trait in the character of American workmen, which is alike detrimental to his pecuniary and social interest. If the employers were to announce at the close of each year's business the amount of their profits during said year, after allowing a proper interest upon their capital, and of said profits were to disburse amongst the employees, say ten or twenty per cent. of said profits, in proportion to the amounts earned by the various workmen, it would tend to make mechanics and laborers more steady and increase their proficiency, and lead them to study the interests of their employers, which would, by this system, become identical with their own. A system of that kind can be inaugurated only by a more fraternal relationship being cultivated between the respective parties, than at present exists. No one will deny that such a system would be conducive to mutual interests; it would be more in accordance with the institutions of our country.

It would have a tendency to counteract the degrading influence of the present system, which is nothing more or less than the same which has been in vogue in the old world since time immemorial. To see the same adopted in America, as the *only* system by which capital and labor can exist, is to acknowledge that, though politically free, we are yet in social bondage, and groping our way through life in deep darkness; and this in the middle of the nineteenth century. If it be objected that the proposed distribution of a portion of the profits will lead to inconvenience, or to dishonest reports on the part of employers; let it be borne in mind that, under the present system the laborer gets none of the profits; he could get no less; and as for inconvenience, it weighs nothing in the scale of justice. If, to secure justice, it becomes necessary to invoke the aid of legislative enactments, let us, in the majesty, and in the right of labor, demand them. Let us have a system of compensation for labor in America, that will bear the imprint of progress; one, the result of which will be to lead the creator of wealth to the enjoyment of at least a portion of his creation.

" I cannot ask for the foregoing suggestion, at the present time, more than a passing notice, but desire it to be recalled at your leisure, that it may be weighed, and, if found correct, its agitation commenced at an early day."—*Extract from Annual Report of the President of International Union of Machinists and Blacksmiths.*

The abandonment of the true interests of society, as embodied in the prosperity of its industrial classes, to the sole influence of a competitive system of wages, is, in its ultimate results, a most injurious omission; it is an exaltation of the element of necessity, to the place of supreme authority in business affairs. The ideas contained in the words " it must needs be," will undoubtedly continue to have an influence in ordinary, as by irresistible decree, they do in the profoundest experiences of life; but the advancing years bring the happiest omens, that their hard features are to be relieved by the genial influence of truths hitherto unnoticed or unrecognized.

Not forgetful in these pages, of the many beneficial results of our present industry, I cannot conceal from myself the burdens which hinder its progress. The distribution of the results of labor seem to me to bear no just proportion to the means of production, the patient application of the toilers, their average elevation of character, as evinced in the sublime deeds of the times, or their social needs.

Our charitable and reformatory institutions, grapple ineffectively with misery and crime; we already propose to limit further effort in this direction. Our extended railroad system, and our projected lines of ocean steamers, indicate a growth as local, and in some respects, as barren as the civilization of mediæval Venice or Genoa; while the occasional wholesale exodus of our people, reveals the industrial burdens under which we labor; we shudder at ancient systems, which have condemned to celibacy, large numbers of human beings, and buried knowledge in dead languages; but fail to see, in the disproportion of the sexes, and the stinted culture of the laboring masses, that we bear the same burdens. The remedy will not be found, until, by a wiser system of abbreviated labor, we faithfully conserve those material, intellectual and moral forces, which the Creator has so bountifully bestowed upon us. In the equation of time proposed by the present reform, we have a proposition, richly charged with germinal influences of future good, paving the way for the development of new productive forces; for the equitable distribution of wealth, and solving, by these means, social problems which have hitherto perplexed the ages.

CONCLUSION.

I recommend as the result of my investigations, and in view of the expressed wish of the interest of labor in the factories, and, so far as ascertained, on the farms; the enactment of ten hours, as a legal standard for a day's labor—in the absence of contracts—for factory and farm work; and a similar enactment of eight hours as a legal standard—in the absence of contracts—for mechanical labor.

Respectfully submitted by

EDWARD H. ROGERS,
Commissioner on the Hours of Labor.

Printed in Dunstable, United Kingdom